Pearls To Purpose

A 90-Day Woman's Guide to Self-Discovery

DOREEN ELLIS

Imani,

You are God's prized possession. Never underestimate your worth. Enjoy the journey. Your purpose awaits.

Love,
Breen

Praise For Pearls...

"This is a pearl of great price!" Doreen Ellis, has gifted the world with a formidable collection of pearls from the crucible of life and keen observation. Her aggregation of gems coupled with Scriptures offers women a three-months supply of blueprints for discovering, revealing, and sculpting the BEST of oneself."

Pastor Phyllis Hilliard
Cathedral International

"If you are seeking to find yourself and your way to life's purpose, Doreen's *Pearls to Purpose* will help you get there. The author inspires with pearls of Godly wisdom to help you take a look at you and your journey. I especially enjoyed the aspirations and personal testaments about how these insights have impacted her journey which encourages you to see how they can be helpful to you. I recommend anyone willing to do the work to gain spiritual clarity of purpose to incorporate this book into their daily devotional activities."

Rochelle Arnold-Simmons
Spiritual Life and Leadership Coach

"Doreen Ellis' *Pearls To Purpose: A 90-Day Woman's Guide To Self-Discovery* is a powerful collection of wisdom designed to inspire the reader in a way that leads them to understand their value. The layout of the book and scriptural references makes it a great tool for everyday use. I love how Doreen has included affirmations that connect the mind, body and soul. May every reader draw closer to God by understanding that they are a masterpiece, fearfully and wonderfully made by Him and designed for a great purpose."

Sonia Jackson Myles
Founder & CEO, The Sister Accord®

"This book and its "Pearls" of wisdom shift your life from bad to good or great to greater. No matter where you are on your journey of life, this book guides you to another level of divine wisdom. Doreen's Godly insight on our purpose is a gift to all of us."

Twyler L. Jenkins
President and Chief Strategist
Strategic Events Solutions, Inc.

"*Pearls to Purpose: A 90-Day Woman's Guide to Self-Discovery* is a jewel! A must-read for the woman who is on the journey to becoming who God called her to be and living the life she was created to live. This is a personal intimate conversation with God, your Father. You will be empowered by God's inspired word to walk in victory."

Yolanda Caldwell
Founder, The Heightening and
Host of The Heightening Podcast

Copyright 2021 by Doreen Ellis. All Rights Reserved.

No part of this book may be reproduced or transmitted in any form or by any means, electronic or mechanical, including photocopying and recording, or by any information storage and retrieval system, without written permission from the author and publisher.

Unless otherwise noted, Scripture quotations are taken from *Holy Bible: The New King James Version*. 1982. Nashville: Thomas Nelson.

Printed in the United States of America
2021 First Edition 10 9 8 7 6 5 4 3 2 1
Subject Index:
Ellis, Doreen

Title: Pearls to Purpose: A 90-Day Woman's Guide to Self-Discovery
1. Christian Inspiration 2. Christian Women's Devotion
3. Christian Women's Issues 4. Women's Empowerment
5. Christian Self-help 6. Christian Personal Growth

Paperback ISBN: 979-8-985-3063-0-9
Library of Congress Control Number: 2022904457

www.DoreenEllis.net

Dedication

To my Dad, James E. Wells, lovingly known as "Nate," who slipped away before I could complete this book. He instilled in me strength, courage, and integrity. He was the first one to shape my view of myself and the world. He valued my opinion and gave me my voice. He was the best Dad for me.

To women on the path to discovering or rediscovering their purpose for this season of their lives.

Acknowledgments

I want to acknowledge my husband, Dr. Alex Ellis, who supported me throughout this project. He was my sounding board and endured me sharing *every* lesson I encountered while writing this book. I also want to thank our beautiful princess, Autumn, who gave me "Mommy breaks" so I could focus on reading and writing. You have taught me in so many ways how to reimagine and live my life on purpose. There is nothing like family support, and I want you both to know how much I love and treasure you.

As I reflect on my life, there are many who helped to shape me into the woman I am today. Some were close and personal, and others I gleaned from afar. The first person who was able to make such a deposit was my dear Mom, Ruthie Wells. Mom, I thank you for your love, dedication, and your sacrifice over the years. I am because you are.

My late grandmother, Louise Wells, was very instrumental in my life. She was my best friend. My grandmother was a quiet and sweet soul – full of wisdom and grace. She loved gardening. She planted the first seed of God in me at a very young age. My Auntie Barbara Wells watered that seed. She was my first bible school teacher. She taught and modeled the Word of God at home, as well as at church. I watched and admired her over the years. She was smart, classy, and savvy. Her life allowed me to see what was possible. As a result, I went on to teach Sunday School at the age of nine and later as a young adult.

There were many women after that who came to nurture the gifts within me. My fifth-grade teacher, Mrs. Mahoney, was one who played a vital role. Mrs. Mahoney was the Claire Huxtable of my day. She was beautiful, classy, and carried herself with dignity and grace. She recognized my math skills and asked if I could stay after school and teach her daughter, Kelly. As a token of her appreciation, she would reward me with chocolate chip cookies or an ice cream sandwich from the school's cafeteria. She even picked me up one Saturday to take her daughter and me out to lunch and a movie. I went on to have many teachers, but Mrs. Mahoney will always stand out of them all.

Along my journey, I gleaned from some amazing women –Pastor Phyllis Hilliard, Dr. Bernadette Glover, Evangelist Shirley "Mom" Graham, Mom Rosetta Mason, the late Elder Phyllis Foster, the late Mom Beatrice Davis, Mom Ida Barlow, Mom Armeta Ellis, Mother Iona Jenkins, Mother Shirley Davis, and Pastor Mary Searight.

I am grateful for the women who inspired me to dream and pursue my purpose–Ms. Mikki Taylor, Sonia Jackson-Myles, Patrice Washington, Janine Uzzell, Rochelle Arnold-Simmons, Glynnis Woolridge, Bishop Wynell Freeman, Oprah, and Forever First Lady, Michelle Obama. They are my Sheroes! Thank you for your example. Keep making a difference in the world and an indelible impact on the next generation!

Foreword

Pearls to Purpose is not only a guide to living a fulfilled life; it's like having author Doreen Ellis by your side whenever you need to be reminded of the truth of who you are and what God intended in creating you. It's full of takeaways and nudges to assure you that God knew what He was doing when He created you and what He placed in you for such a time as this. We were created to lead fearless, faithful, and empowered lives. Lives that demonstrate that we know our value and, through exemplary living, celebrate and honor body, mind, and spirit. There's no better time than right now to curl up with this book on a daily basis and define what's truly essential for you to thrive. What I know for sure... we cannot provoke much-needed change in the world around us, pour into the next generations, and make a seismic shift in our communities if we're not first a powerful force in our own lives. This calls for an intentional walk and for each of us to be informed, affirmed, and inspired.

I don't like untested advice, which is why I love how the author puts herself on the line regarding these time-honored truths. You'll want to high-five yourself when she talks about the real gratification that comes from investing in yourself is always worth the time – and then gives you scriptures to prove it! In fact, she'll help you set some boundaries, drop any self-imposed guilt, and let you know that not taking the time to self-nurture is at best self-sabotage. The busy mom and wife understands what substantive living is all about, and there's a pearl of wisdom contained herein for taking on every aspect of life. They're all hinged on Biblical power points that urge us to remember *who* and what we're working with, for this is the truth that will sustain us.

For all of you who'll take this journey through this book, you'll also discover why what lies inside of you has the power to motivate or defeat you. The power of our thoughts can either move us forward and ensure that we flourish or hold us back from the joy and success we should embrace. This is one of many reasons why *Pearls* cautions us against self-limiting views and that which doesn't serve us well lest we become collateral damage of our own doing. Recognizing that God created everything with purpose and intent is what has sustained this author, and she whispers to our hearts about the importance of seeing our lives through the lens of His perspective. I say think of it as a soul-selfie so you can grow and glow!

Finally, this is an opportunity to turn the Word and these pearls of wisdom on yourself and tighten up your leadership territory. I kept shaking my head as I read this book and saying yes, yes, and yes. God has placed raw, unfinished, imperfect potential in each of us and every day, it is being perfected and nurtured to maturity. Purpose is about knowing that God is working on something greater than you determined and that no matter the disruption, distraction, or opposition, you will, not maybe, complete that which you have been created to do.

So, if you're ready to give yourself continuous permission to be the *force* that God created, put the phone on silent, get up early if you have to, do whatever it takes to spend time with *Pearls to Purpose*, you'll be so glad you did.

Mikki Taylor
Author, Empowerment Speaker

Table Of Contents

Dedication vi

Acknowledgments vii

Foreword ix

Introduction.. xvii

Pearl #1: The Bible – Our Instruction Manual 1

Pearl #2: Made In His Image 3

Pearl #3: Tailor-Made 5

Pearl #4: Simply Be 7

Pearl #5: Our Nature... 9

Pearl #6: It's in Your DNA.. 11

Pearl #7: You Are Predestined 13

Pearl #8: Follow the Blueprint 15

Pearl #9: Divine Mindset.. 17

Pearl # 10: The Power of a Thought....................................... 19

Pearl #11: I Changed My Mind.. 21

Pearl #12: Mental Wellness... 23

Pearl #13: Self-Discovery.. 25

Pearl #14: Peeling Back the Layers... 27

Pearl #15: Core Values.. 29

Pearl #16: Character – What's in You? 31

Pearl #17: No Guilt, No Shame 33

Pearl #18: Mindful Self-Talk 35

Pearl #19: Know Who You Are 37

Pearl #20: Created to Create 39

Pearl #21: You Are a Gift! 41

Pearl #22: Be Salt 43

Pearl #23: Shine Bright 45

Pearl #24: Hidden Treasure 47

Pearl #25: A Woman of Substance 49

Pearl #26: Complete in Christ 51

Pearl #27: You Are a Masterpiece 53

Pearl #28: I Am Who God Says I Am 55

Pearl #29: Know I'm Not 57

Pearl #30: I Am Loved 59

Pearl #31: I Am Becoming 61

Pearl #32: The Right Kind of Confidence 63

Pearl #33: The Beauty of Authenticity 65

Pearl #34: Imposter Syndrome 67

Pearl #35: Dare to Be Rare 69

Pearl #36: Love Yourself! 71

Pearl #37: Guard Your Heart 73

Pearl #38: Created to Love 75

Pearl #39: Created to Serve 77

Pearl #40: I Am Beautiful 79

Pearl #41: Perfectly Flawed 81

Pearl #42: That's How I'm Wired 83

Pearl #43: What Do You Want? 85

Pearl #44: What Do You Need? 87

Pearl #45: Just Ask 89

Pearl #46: Blind Spots 91

Pearl #47: Seek Within 93

Pearl #48: Speak & Seek 95

Pearl #49: Walk in Truth 97

Pearl #50: Mind Your Business 99

Pearl #51: Step by Step 101

Pearl #52: Deeply Rooted 103

Pearl #53: Made to Prosper 105

Pearl #54: The Tortoise and The Hare 107

Pearl #55: What's the Rush? 109

Pearl #56: Women of Influence 111

Pearl #57: I'm Different 113

Pearl #58: Shall We Dance? 115

Pearl #59: Go with the Flow 117

Pearl #60: Times of Refreshing – Self-Care 119

Pearl #61: Time of Refueling - Self-Care (2) 121

Pearl #62: Preparation Is Key 123

Pearl #63: Perfection is a Myth 125

Pearl #64: I Am Worth It.. 127

Pearl #65: The Unknown.. 129

Pearl #66: The Grace to Forgive... 131

Pearl #67: Let it Go! 133

Pearl #68: To Know Him 135

Pearl #69: The Right Attitude.. 137

Pearl #70: Take Time to Unplug.. 139

Pearl #71: The Art of Stillness.. 141

Pearl #72: The Power of Association 143

Pearl #73: Find Your Tribe 145

Pearl #74: Remember Who You Are 147

Pearl #75: Knowing When to Serve or Be Served 149

Pearl #76: Answer the Call 151

Pearl #77: The Right Balance 153

Pearl #78: Get Wisdom 155

Pearl #79: Full Circle.. 157

Pearl #80: A New Beginning 159

Pearl #81: Be Unstoppable 161

Pearl #82: Choose Contentment 163

Pearl #83: Rejection or Direction?... 165

Pearl #84: Pruning Season 167

Pearl #85: The Master Vinedresser... 169

Pearl #86: The True Vine – Stay Connected... 171

Pearl #87: Do the Work.. 173

Pearl #88: Breakout! 175

Pearl #89: Capacity 177

Pearl #90: Poised & Positioned for Purpose 179

Appendix A: Self-Discovery: Getting to Know You Exercise 181

Appendix – B: The Power of Affirmations 183

Resources 185

About The Author 186

Introduction

Every manufacturer provides instructions on how to use a product. If we want to maximize the fullest use of a product, we must READ THE INSTRUCTIONS. These instructions are usually found inside the package in BIG BOLD print. But how many are like me, who want to jump in and start trying to figure it out by looking at the finished picture on the box?

If we're honest, that is how the majority of us operate. Who has time to read all of the preliminaries before using a product? It seems to be a big waste of time.

I can't count how many times I was going through something in my life or just needed direction in a particular area, and the Lord would guide me to Scripture, or I would see a word that reminded me of a story in the Bible.

The Bible is like an atlas filled with maps, keys, and legends. The Word recounts where we came from, who we are and why we are here. It's our roadmap and contains the answers we will need to navigate through the journey of life!

> *This Book of the Law shall not depart from your mouth, but you shall meditate in it day and night, that you may observe to do according to all that is written in it. For then you will make your way prosperous, and then you will have good success.* **–Joshua 1:8**

If you are longing to find your purpose, I encourage you to read the Word (the Bible, our Manual for living) and allow God to show you His plan for your life. (Jeremiah 29:11)

God is our manufacturer, and His instructions are found in His Word. We must take time to READ the instructions if we desire to reach our fullest potential.

Pearls

Throughout the book, I will share the wisdom I have gleaned from Scripture on my personal journey. I refer to these truths as Pearls. I like to think of wisdom as Pearls – priceless gems that are produced in maturity.

A pearl is not produced until it is agitated. When a foreign substance slips between the mantle and an oyster shell, it naturally reacts by covering up and protecting itself in nacre. Nacre is an organic compound material produced in the layer of the inner surface of a shell. This material is very strong, resilient, and iridescent—earning the name "Mother of Pearl."

Interestingly, all pearls are not created equal—the shape and authenticity of a pearl matter. Naturally cultured pearls are perfectly round and smooth. These pearls are known for their fine quality and are considered rare, fine, admirable, and valuable.

The Greatest Creator of all time designed the world in a perfect sphere. He engineered everything to come full circle. Our thoughts and habits shape how we see ourselves and how we view the world. Just look *"a-round,"* and you will see.

God is intentional. When He created you, He saw you whole and complete—lacking nothing. Whether you are on the path to discovering or rediscovering who you are, this book is designed to help you get there. I share pearls that will guide you to living a well-rounded life. As you explore the pages, I pray that you will see yourself as God sees you; live a life fulfilling purpose; then reach back and empower others to do the same.

Additional resources can be found at the end of the book to help guide you along the journey. Now, let's get ready to explore! Enjoy the venture!

PEARL #1

The Bible – Our Instruction Manual

*In the beginning, was the Word, and the Word
was with God, and the Word was God.*
John 1:1

*"God's Word has the power to light our way and to clear
the debris that has covered the path so we can walk in it."*
–Lisa Bevere

The Word of God is eternal. It is amazing how we can read a particular book or verse in the Bible one season of our lives and get one understanding. Then read that same passage in another season and get a completely different revelation. The Word didn't change; our perception did.

Often, when we don't understand something, our natural reaction is to dismiss it. But if we apply our hearts to instruction and diligently search the Manual, not only do we find answers; light comes. We begin to see life through the lens of our Creator. We come to know the origin of His intent.

We are continually evolving, but God knows everything about us. He had purpose in mind when He designed us. There is no facet in life that will take our Creator by surprise. What may seem complicated to us is not complicated to Him. His ways are not our ways. (Isaiah 55:8)

With all the turns, roadblocks, and detours in my life there is one thing that has remained constant – The Word of God. It helped me to discover that life is not happening to me, it is happening for me. (Romans 8:28)

When life presents you with challenges, and you are unsure what to do, check the Manual. The BIBLE is Basic Instructions Before Leaving Earth. It contains the answers to anything life may bring.

The BIBLE = Basic Instructions Before Leaving Earth

Affirmation: I delight in reading God's word. It gives me insight into how to live life and reach my fullest potential here on earth.

Scripture References
Isaiah 55:8-9
Psalms 139:16
Proverbs 23:12
Matthew 10:30
John 1:1
Romans 8:28

PEARL #2

Made In His Image

God created man in His own image; in the image of God He created him; male and female He created them.
Genesis 1:27

"Life isn't about finding yourself, it's about discovering who God created you to be."
–Anonymous

Do you realize how precious you are in the sight of God? After creating all that He made, He desired fellowship. On the sixth day, He created man in His own image. He formed us from the dust of the ground, then breathed into us the breath of life and we became a living being.

Our purpose on earth is to have continual fellowship with our Creator. God's intent is for us to reflect His image and likeness. Our primary role is to be fruitful and multiply; fill the earth and subdue it. He created us to have dominion over the fish of the sea and the birds of the air and over every living thing that moves on the earth.

Life began to change for me when I allowed Genesis 1 to read me, as opposed to me reading it. This very familiar Scripture took on new form and began to shape how I saw myself. I realized we are His representatives. We have the awesome privilege of walking with God and exercising our authority on His behalf.

Jesus perfectly demonstrated this during His time on earth. When Phillip asked Jesus to show him the Father, He replied, "He who has seen Me has seen the Father…" (John 14:9) After Jesus ascended into Heaven, He sent His Spirit to dwell among those who believed in Him. We have been crucified with Christ; it is no longer we who live, but Christ lives in us; and the life we now live in the flesh we live by faith in the Son of God, who loved us and gave Himself for us. (Galatians 2:20)

Affirmation: I am created in God's image. Christ lives in me. I am His re-presentative in the earth.

Scripture References
Genesis 1:27
John 14:9
John 14:12
Galatians 2:20

PEARL #3

Tailor-Made

*You formed my inward parts; You covered me in my mother's womb.
I will praise You, for I am fearfully and wonderfully made;
Marvelous are Your works, and that my soul knows very well.*
Psalm 139:13-14

*"Tailors were created for a reason.
Every suit is not designed to fit you."*
Doreen Ellis

My husband and I enjoy watching the TV series *Project Runway*. We love to see how designers use their creative abilities to transform garments using their unique talents. What's more exciting is how they tailor each piece in such a way that is flattering for each model. These designers are great, however there is One who is greater. I am amazed at how multifaceted God is. Every intricate part of our being is fashioned by Him. Out of an estimated 7.8 billion people on the earth, He uniquely designed each one of us. God is a God of details. He doesn't make mistakes. Even the very hairs on our head are numbered. (Luke 12:7) He tailored us in such a way that no one else can fit our suit.

God not only shaped and formed our outer parts, He intentionally crafted our inward parts. He knows how we are wired. He knows our thoughts and intentions. Everything that we need to fulfill our purpose has been placed within us.

God knew exactly what He had in mind when He made us. He placed within us special gifts, talents and abilities to benefit ourselves and others. On this path to purpose journey, I realized people spend a lifetime seeking to discover who they are. The truth is, God desires to show us. As we seek Him, the nature of our being is revealed and His very purpose for our lives unfold.

Affirmation: Every fiber of my being is distinctly fashioned by my Creator. I am tailor-made with intentionality.

Scripture References
I Chronicles 28:9
Jeremiah 29:13
Psalms 139:13-14
Luke 12:7

PEARL #4

Simply Be

*When I consider Your heavens, the work of Your fingers,
The moon, and the stars, which You have ordained,
What is man that You are mindful of him…*
Psalm 8:3-4

One spring afternoon, I was outdoors enjoying nature when I noticed a big beautiful tree. Its branches extended far and wide with leaves that adorned every limb. I watched as birds flew back and forth, looking to find a particular place to lodge, and the squirrels played chase around its long trunk.

Trees are the biggest plant on the earth and a vital source to our environment. They take in carbon dioxide and provide the oxygen we breathe. They filter the water we drink, stabilize the soil and give life to the wildlife. It's amazing how essential the role of a tree is by simply being.

If God is intentional about the purpose of a tree, how much more is He about the purpose of humanity? God created everything with purpose and intent. There is an assignment for everything on the face of the earth. We all have an individual role to play.

There is nothing more frustrating than seeing someone trying to operate in an area they were not created to function. Have you ever seen a tree trying to be a flower or the moon trying to be the sun? Their sole purpose is to function in the area they were designed to function. Humans are the only species that try to function outside of purpose.

We can learn many lessons from a tree. In fact, the Bible uses many metaphors of a tree to give us insight into how we should conduct our lives. Take a look at Psalm 1:3, "He should be like a tree planted by the rivers of water, that brings forth fruit in its season…" Trees stand tall. They are deeply rooted and can weather the storm. The mere existence of trees brings life to all living species. God made everything for a specific purpose. We don't reserve the right to alter it to suit our preferences. Just look at the nature of a tree. Oh, how joyful life can be if we learn to simply be.

*"The Bible is God's revelation of Himself to us,
and it is our most reliable source of His nature and purposes."*
Dr. Myles Munroe

Affirmation: Wherever I am planted, I will grow because I was made to flourish. I am learning to simply be.

Scripture References
Jeremiah 17:8
Psalms 1:3
Psalms 8:3-4
Acts 17:27-28
Romans 12:4

PEARL #5

Our Nature

*For as by one man's disobedience many were made sinners,
so also by one Man's obedience, many will be made righteous.*
Romans 5:19

Sin entered the world through the first man, Adam. Unfortunately, his sinful nature was passed down to us, and we inherited that same nature. We are all born sinners, whether we choose to accept it or not. But the good news is, Christ came to earth to bear the sins of the world so that we may be made righteous in Him.

When we accept Christ Jesus into our lives, we come into the family of God. We take on Christ's nature, and we become God's children. "If anyone be in Christ, he is a new creation; old things have passed away; behold, all things have become new." (2 Corinthians 5:17) No longer are we bound by our former nature. "There is therefore now no condemnation to those who are in Christ Jesus." (Romans 8:1) It is through grace we are saved and forgiven. For the law of the spirit of life in Christ Jesus has made us free from the law of sin and death. (Romans 8:2)

We are Kingdom citizens who live not according to the flesh but according to the Spirit. And the kingdom of God is righteousness, peace, and joy in the Holy Spirit. That is our birthright.

Affirmation: I am the righteousness of God. I am a Kingdom citizen. It's my birthright.

Scripture References
Romans 5:17
Romans 8:1-17
Romans 14:17
2 Corinthians 5:17

PEARL #6

It's in Your DNA

Then God said, "Let Us make man in Our image, according to Our likeness…"
Genesis 1:26

"Your spiritual DNA is perfect. Your only limits are those you impose on yourself."
Bob Proctor

The true origin of any species can be found in its DNA. It's not by chance that you see renowned singers have children who grow up with the natural ability to sing. DNA is a molecule that carries biological instructions from one generation to the next. I like to refer to it as our **D**istinct **N**atural **A**bility.

We were created in God's image and His likeness. Unfortunately, after the fall of man, sin entered the human race. The Good News is Christ came to redeem us from the curse of sin and death. We have the right to redemption once we acknowledge Christ and ask Him to come into our hearts. Once that occurs, we are regenerated. The Spirit of God resides in us, and we have His DNA. The sooner we realize this, the sooner we can operate on earth as He originally designed.

Before the earth was framed, God created by speaking things into existence, and since we have His DNA, we have the distinct ability to do the same. That's why it is so important that we watch what we say.

"Death and life are in the power of the tongue…" (Proverbs 18:21). Our words have power. They are a mighty force that can cause good and harm. When we speak, all creation comes together to make it happen. It's in our DNA.

I recall when I was seeking direction in my new career path and my spiritual mother asked, "What do you want to do?" I told her, "I want to write." As I took the necessary steps and began writing, it wasn't long before I received an offer to be a contributing writer for a Women's Empowerment newsletter. That led me to writing this book. There is power in our declaration!

Now that we know this, let us set a guard over our mouths; keep watch of the doors of our lips, and choose our words wisely.

Affirmation: I was born to create. It's my DNA. My words have power. I choose my words wisely.

Scripture References
Genesis 1:3
Psalm 19:14
Psalms 141:3
Proverbs 18:21
Mark 11:23
Ephesians 4:29

PEARL #7

You Are Predestined

*For whom He foreknew, He also predestined
to be conformed to the image of His Son…*
Romans 8:28

*"When you present yourself to life as a serious student,
life will respond by providing you with an endless opportunity
to learn and grow and develop, and enhance any
and all aspects of your life."*
Jim Rohn

Despite how you came into this world, you were meant to be. You were predestined. God knew you before your mother met your daddy. He generated your DNA and knew precisely the right time for you to step on the scene. The fact that you are here means there is a purpose for your existence.

When we seek our Creator and align with His purpose, His plan for our lives begins to unfold. This is a continual process. As we grow and evolve, we will learn and discover. "But let patience have its perfect work…" (James 1:4) Allow Him to have His way. "He predestined us for adoption to himself as sons through Jesus Christ, according to the purpose of His will." (Ephesians 1:5)

We are on divine assignment. There is a specific task that God has in mind for each of us. It is our responsibility to discover what that is and work toward fulfilling it.

Make no mistake: "Whom He predestined, these He also called; whom He called, these He also justified; and whom He justified, these He also glorified." (Romans 8:30) You are part of God's plan, and you are destined to fulfill your purpose.

Affirmation: I am predestined by God, and no force on earth is powerful enough to stop me from pursuing my purpose.

Scripture References
Romans 8:29-30
Ephesians 1:5
James 1:4

PEARL #8

Follow the Blueprint

Keep your eyes on those who live as we do.
Philippians 3:17

"And when you discover what you will be in life, set out to do it as if God Almighty called you at this particular moment in history to do it. Set out to do such a good job that the living, the dead or the unborn couldn't do it any better."
Dr. Martin Luther King Jr.

Jesus is the blueprint for the life of a believer. His sole purpose was to do the work of the Father. During His brief time on earth, he modeled how to walk in oneness with the Father. He was focused. He was intentional. He didn't allow anything to dissuade Him from His purpose. He lived to carry out His assignment and to bring God glory, and He did it perfectly.

We were all created with a purpose, and it is our responsibility to fulfill our assignment on earth. This will not come without your share of challenges and opposition. However, don't allow the distractions of life to deter you from pursuing your mission. Be steadfast, immovable, always abounding in the work of the Lord.

When distractions come, refer to the blueprint. Jesus came so that we may have a model. If we follow the blueprint, we can't lose. Paul shared these words with the Philippians, "Join together in following my example, brothers and sisters, and just as you have us as a model, keep your eyes on those who live as we do." (Philippians 3:17) In essence, Paul was saying, follow me as I follow Christ.

Affirmation: I was designed with a plan in mind and the necessary tools to win.

Scripture References
1 Corinthians 11:1
Philippians 3:17
Hebrews 13:7
I Peter 2:21

PEARL #9

Divine Mindset

Be transformed by the renewing of your mind…
Romans 12:2

"When the mind is renewed we transform. The limited becomes limitless. We are able to break out and make room for expansion."
Doreen Ellis

Our finite minds pale in comparison to how God sees us in the world. When our minds are renewed, we are able to see life through the lens of God's perspective. We see life through a glass dimly, but God sees the full view. (1 Corinthians 13:12) But as we trust Him, lean not on our understanding, and fully commit our ways to Him, He will direct our paths. (Proverbs 3:6)

We are constantly evolving, so we must renew our minds daily. Being careful to cast down imaginations and any thoughts that do not align with the Word. (2 Corinthians 10:5) I like to take time each morning to get quiet before God; meditate on His Word, and journal. It allows me to clear my mind from clutter.

I encourage you to designate time each day for a moment of quietness. Develop the art of listening. It's only when we are still that we can truly hear and think clearly. When we take time to renew our minds, we awaken our imagination. Creative ideas began to flow. We gain a fresh perspective, allowing transformation to take place.

*"The mind, once stretched by a new idea,
never returns to its original dimensions."*
Ralph Waldo Emerson

Affirmation: My mind, body, and spirit are in divine alignment. I choose to view life from God's perspective, not my own.

Scripture References
Psalm 46:10
Proverbs 3:5-6
Romans 12:2
I Corinthians 13:12
II Corinthians 10:5

PEARL # 10

The Power of a Thought

*Whatever things are true, whatever things are noble,
whatever things are just, whatever things
are pure… meditate on these things.*
Philippians 4:8

You are the sum total of your thoughts. The average person thinks up to 6,200 thoughts a day. It is impossible to entertain that many thoughts. So why do some stay while others vanish like the wind? The fact that the word "thought" is mentioned over 100 times in the Bible indicates that you should take your thoughts seriously. Growing up, I recall hearing an expression, "A penny for your thoughts." I now realize that thoughts can be quite expensive.

Your thoughts frame the way you live and view life, whether good or bad. Thoughts are so powerful that they can change the condition of a thing just by how you choose to think about it. If you think negatively, your outcome will be negative. But if you choose to allow the negative thought to pass through, you will discover there are plenty of other thoughts floating in your mind. You can choose a good one at any given time. (Philippians 4:8)

Think about the television and the many channels it offers. If you don't care for the program, you can switch to another channel. That's true for your thoughts as well. Your mind is the television, and your thoughts are the channels. You have the authority to cast down arguments and every high thing that exalts itself against the knowledge of God, and bring every thought into captivity to the obedience of Christ. (2 Corinthians 10:5) Get into the habit of praying this Scripture daily as it helps to redirect your negative thoughts.

The happiness of your life depends upon the quality of your thoughts. Never underestimate the power of your thoughts.

Affirmation: I have the power to channel my thoughts. Every cell in my body vibrates with positive energy.

Scripture References
Jeremiah 17:9-10
Philippians 2:5
Philippians 4:8
2 Corinthians 10:5

PEARL #11

I Changed My Mind

Be not conformed to this world: but be ye transformed by the renewing of your mind...
Romans 12:2

"You have the right to change your mind."
Oprah Winfrey

Your mind is a gateway to your soul. Where the mind goes, the body follows. According to the Merriam-Webster dictionary, a gate is a moveable barrier, a means of entrance or exit. A gateway typically has hinges that can swing open or closed. A closed gate can represent a barrier for anything trying to go out, and an open gate can represent access for anything trying to come in.

There are three gates that make up your thought process: the ear gate, the mind gate, and the heart gate. What enters into each gate helps to form your subconscious belief system. These thought patterns begin as early as childhood, and if you are not careful, they become barriers that hinder you from moving forward.

I'm sure you can remember one negative thing that a family member or teacher said to you that warped your way of thinking. The person may not even recall what they said, but you still carry the trauma to this day. The hardest prison to escape is the mind. If you are ever going to break free from your old way of thinking, you must choose to change your mind. (1 Corinthians 13:11)

The beautiful thing about the mind is that you can create a new thought process that aligns with your divine purpose. You do not have to conform to the world's way of thinking. When negative thoughts come, replace them with those that line up with the Word of truth. Let the Word be a filter as to what you let in and what to let out. Make sure that you mind the gates of your heart with all diligence because out of your heart flows the issues of life.

Affirmation: I align my thoughts with the Word of truth. I am being transformed daily by the renewing of my mind.

Scripture References
Proverbs 4:23-27
Romans 12:2
1 Corinthians 2:13-15
1 Corinthians 13:11
Philippians 2:5

PEARL #12

Mental Wellness

"Do you want to be made well?"
John 5:6

"Live from the inside out. Your mind, body, and spirit are interconnected. Nourish your soul with mental and physical wellness."
Janet Taylor Spence

God is concerned about your physical and mental wellness. I was having a session with my life coach about things that drain me when she challenged me to dig deeper. She asked me, "Why do you feel that way?" I didn't have any words. I had no idea why I was allowing my outside circumstances to determine my internal disposition.

After some soul-searching, it hit me that there is no perfect situation. There will always be circumstances beyond my control. However, I can control how I choose to let it affect me. It's all about perspective.

In John 5, there was a man who had an illness for 38 years. The text doesn't specify the exact condition, but it does state that he laid at the pool, which most conclude was a physical condition. At any rate, Jesus saw him lying there by the "Sheep Gate" pool (also known as Bethesda). Jesus asked him, "Do you want to be made well?" (John 5:6) Instead of addressing the question, the man responded with excuses for why he was still in his current condition. The man's response appears to show that his illness was more than physical; it was also mental.

Like the man lying by the pool, often we are so caught up in our systematic way of thinking that we make excuses for things we are not ready to change. It may take someone on the outside to expose these areas in our lives, but we must be open to receiving help. We can't fix what we don't face. Wellness begins when you stop making excuses and start making moves.

Affirmation: Wellness is a choice. I am well. I am healthy. I am healed. I am free–mentally and physically.

Scripture References
Luke 14:18-20
John 5:1-9
Romans 12:1-2

PEARL #13

Self-Discovery

*"You have hidden these things from the wise and learned,
and revealed them to little children."*
Matthew 11:25 (NIV)

*"Whatever stimulates you and pushes you to be
at your best must be realized."*
Mikki Taylor

With each new stage of life, you will discover more and more about yourself. Our lives are filled with adventures that allow opportunities for self-discovery.

I love to watch children play. Their creative imaginations grow as they play. They have the most inquisitive minds. It's amazing to see how their personalities develop at such a young age. Some are curious, some are quiet, some are spontaneous, and others are reserved.

Little children do not fear exploring because the only limits they know are the ones we put on them. Can you imagine a life without limits? Endless possibilities await us if we are willing to reach beyond our grasp. This is only possible when we release the little child in us. It's where all consciousness of ourselves and of what God is doing through us is eliminated. Our dependence is solely on Him, and we are available to do whatever He wants us to do.

Just like children play to learn, adults need to learn to play. We can be childlike without being childish. Make time for play and discover the child in you.

> *"We are all meant to shine, as children do. It is not just in some of us; it is in everyone, and as we let our light shine, we unconsciously give others permission to do the same."*
> ***Marianne Williamson***

Affirmation: Each day is a brand new opportunity to discover the child in me. I am free to explore and experience a life without limits.

Scripture References
Psalm 119:18-20
Matthew 18:3
Mark 10:13-16
Acts 12:11
Ephesians 5:1-2

PEARL #14

Peeling Back the Layers

*I invite your searching gaze into my heart.
Examine me through and through;
find out everything that may be hidden within me.*
Psalm 139:23 (TPT)

*"When you first start off trying to solve a problem, the first solutions
you come up with are very complex, and most people stop there.
But if you keep going and live with the problem and peel
more layers of the onion off, you can often time arrive at
some very elegant and simple solutions."*
Steve Jobs

An onion has so many intricate layers. With every layer that is peeled back, another layer is revealed. Life is much like an onion. The layers of our lives are tightly sealed. We close ourselves off to others, trying to keep our secret parts from being exposed. When an onion is cut, it releases a stench that will make the toughest person cry. The same is true of us. It may appear that we have it all together on the outside, but deep down inside, some things stink.

Peeling back the layers requires vulnerability. It's a very uncomfortable place as it begins to open up areas in our lives that we have to face. But if we want to be whole, we must open up and get to the heart of the matter. Brené Brown states, "Staying vulnerable is a risk we have to take if we want to experience connection."

If the layers of your life were peeled back, what would they reveal? Would there be bitterness, guilt, insecurity, low self-esteem, envy, or jealousy? We don't like to talk about the layers of our lives. We would rather keep them hidden–settling for a surface life, representing the ideal person we want people to perceive us to be.

I can assure you that no one is exempt from this process. We all have areas in our lives, if they were cut open, would wreak a foul stench. Allow God to peel back the layers of your facade. Invite Him into the stinky areas of your life. He wants to heal your internal wounds and replace them with His sweet aroma.

Affirmation: I am peeling back the layers of my life one layer at a time. Every layer leads to healing and revealing the inner me.

Scripture References
Psalm 139:23-24
Psalm 147:3
Romans 8:27

PEARL #15

Core Values

Then God said, "Let the land produce vegetation: seed-bearing plants and trees on the land that bear fruit with seed in it, according to their various kinds." And it was so.
Genesis 11:1

"Your core values are deeply held beliefs that authentically describe your soul."
John C. Maxwell

Everything God intended to reproduce started in seed form. The origin of a thing can be determined by its core. Apple seeds produce apples. Orange seeds produce oranges, and watermelon seeds produce watermelon.

Just as fruit has a core, our bodies have a core. Our core is an essential part of the body. It keeps us centered. When it is strengthened, it leads to better posture, balance, and flexibility.

In a spiritual sense, our core values keep us aligned with our purpose. It allows us to identify the things that are most important to us. When we are clear on our core values, we will find it easier to say "No" to the things that do not serve us and "Yes" to the things that bring us true fulfillment.

My core values are family, freedom, integrity and well-being. I take into consideration all of these things when I need to make a decision. It's important for me to honor my core values because it helps me to show up as my true authentic-self.

Who are you at the core? What do you value? When you answer these questions, this is where you need to devote your time, money, and energy. The more you strengthen your core, the better you will be mentally, physically, and spiritually. It's the key to well-being.

Affirmation: I am centered. My mind, body, and spirit are in complete alignment with my core values.

Scripture References
Genesis 11:1
Genesis 15:2-6
Proverbs 22:1
Matthew 6:21

PEARL #16

Character – What's in You?

There is nothing that enters a man from outside which can defile him; but the things which come out of him, those are the things that defile a man.
Mark 7:15

"Crises reveal character. When we are put to the test the hidden resources of our character are revealed exactly."
Oswald Chambers

As a little child, I remember a classic nursery rhyme titled, "What Are Little Girls Made Of?" It goes on to say, "Sugar and spice and everything nice. That's what little girls are made of." This is what I was led to believe when I was growing up. But as I continued to grow, I began to realize we are made of so much more.

No one is born with character. It is one area that is continually being developed. Our life experiences help to shape our distinctive qualities and values. These habits and traits form our personalities and, ultimately, our reputation. However, true character is only revealed under pressure. It's not until we are squeezed that we truly know what we are made of.

Think about it, if you squeeze a tube of toothpaste, you'll get toothpaste. If you squeeze a lemon, you'll get lemon juice. Now ask yourself, "What would someone get if they squeezed me? The truth is, whatever is inside of you will eventually come out. For out of the abundance of the heart, the mouth speaks. (Matthew 12:34)

Character is not just what we see on the outside; it's who we are when no one is looking. What you do in the dark will eventually come to light. As Christians, your "inner life" should be a reflection of a life hidden in Christ. Your "outer life" is the expressed life that makes Christ known to others.

Affirmation: I am an outward expression of an inward life hidden in Christ.

Scripture References
Matthew 12:34
Mark 7:15
Mark 7:20
Isaiah 29:15

PEARL #17

No Guilt, No Shame

The Lord God helps me; therefore I have not been disgraced;
therefore I have set my face like a flint, and I know
that I shall not be put to shame.
Isaiah 50:7

We often use the words guilt and shame synonymously. But the two are quite different. A person who operates in shame has too much pride to admit their shortcomings or wrongdoings. They like to cover up or blame someone else for their negligence to keep from being exposed. However, a person who operates in guilt personally feels responsible for their actions or the lack thereof. They own their faults and do what they can to make it right.

Since the beginning of time, we see shame in operation. After Adam and Eve ate the fruit of the tree, their eyes were enlightened. And as they heard the sound of God walking in the garden, they sought to cover themselves because they were naked and ashamed. (Genesis 3:8) When pride comes, then comes shame. (Proverbs 11:2) Shame is an unpleasant thought that involves a negative evaluation of yourself. Adam and Eve knew they were wrong, and they tried to hide from God. Even when He confronted them, they made excuses instead of telling the truth.

However, David was a man after God's own heart. He was far from perfect, but when he sinned, he was quick to confess his sins and prayed to God, "Create in me a clean heart, and renew the right spirit within me." (Psalm 51:10) David's heart was sincere, and as a result, God forgave him.

God does not want us to walk in guilt or shame. He desires for us to walk uprightly before Him. He loves us and stands ready to show His grace when we acknowledge our sins.

Affirmation: I am forgiven and set free from the weight of guilt and shame. I choose to walk in God's grace.

Scripture References
Genesis 2:25
Genesis 3:8
Isaiah 50:7
Proverbs 11:2
2 Corinthians 4:2
Roman 5:15-17
1 John 1:5-10

PEARL #18

Mindful Self-Talk

Whatever things are true, whatever things are noble, whatever things are just, whatever things are pure, whatever things are lovely, whatever things are of good report…meditate on these things.
Philippians 4:8

"Don't be a victim of negative self-talk -- remember YOU are listening."
Bob Proctor

While we live in a world with so much negativity, we must be extremely mindful of our thoughts. Our words and thoughts dominate our lives. Life and death are in the power of the tongue. (Proverbs 18:21) Our words have the ability to empower or imprison us. (Proverbs 6:2) So it's important to address this habit we all have, commonly known as "self-talk."

Self-talk is a monologue we have with ourselves. It is a combination of our inner voice, conscious thoughts, and subconscious beliefs. These thoughts can be positive and uplifting or negative and self-destructive. Studies have found that most of our inner thoughts are negative, which means we often talk ourselves out of a good situation. But it is also possible to talk ourselves into a good one.

We rise or fall to the level of our confession. However, it is not enough to declare words. We must have faith to believe that we receive before we can have it. (Mark 11:24) Faith is the ability to confess what we don't yet possess. (Hebrews 11:1)

The woman who had an issue for twelve years not only spoke to herself, but she believed if she could just touch the hem of Jesus' garment, she would be made whole. (Matthew 9:21) David encouraged himself in the Lord when he was deeply depressed, and men sought to stone him to death. (1 Samuel 30:6) Then he sought the Lord in prayer, pursued his enemy, and recovered all that was lost. (1 Samuel 30:19)

What are you saying to yourself? The stories you tell yourself make you who you are. It matters not what others say about you; it's what you say to yourself.

Affirmation: I am my best cheerleader. I choose to think and speak those things that edify, encourage, and empower myself and others.

Scripture References
1 Samuel 30:6
1 Samuel 30:19
Matthew 9:21
Mark 11:24
Hebrews 11:1
Philippians 4:8

PEARL #19

Know Who You Are

You are a chosen generation, a royal priesthood, a holy nation…
1 Peter 2:9

"When you know yourself you are empowered.
When you accept yourself you are invincible."
Tina Lifford

Knowing who you are is so liberating. You're not trying to fit in, nor are you comparing yourself to anyone else's standard. You are a Designer's original, not a carbon copy. You are clear on your purpose and don't accept anything contrary to that.

When you know who you are, you will come to realize you are not meant for everyone, and everyone is not meant for you. Jesus did not waste time trying to convince people who He was. Even the few times He did, they didn't believe.

God made you unique, and you are one of a kind. Embrace your uniqueness and allow God to mold and shape you into the individual He has designed you to be.

Nobody can beat you, being YOU! Don't forfeit the opportunity of being the best you, YOU, can be!

YOU = Your Own Uniqueness

Be original, not a knock-off! Seek God (your Manufacturer) and ask Him to reveal the true essence of who you are.

Affirmation: I know who I am. I own my uniqueness. I am becoming all that God designed me to be.

Scripture References
2 Corinthians 6:17
Galatians 5:1
Ephesians 2:10
1 Peter 2:9

PEARL #20

Created to Create

For we are God's handiwork, created in Christ Jesus to do good works, which God prepared in advance for us to do.
Ephesians 2:10

*"Life is not about what you are given,
it's about what you create."*
Anonymous

God designed you to be creative in His creation. I once heard a story about a man who needed a table, and God provided a tree. God supplies the raw materials, but it is up to you to create. God told Noah to build an ark. Do you think Noah had a clue about how to make an ark? But God did. He placed inside Noah the necessary tools to get the job done. And Noah did everything just as God commanded him. (Genesis 6:22)

Oswald Chambers states, "The one true mark of a saint of God is the inner creativity that flows from being surrendered to Jesus Christ."

I discovered that I am most creative when I write. I come alive with a pen and paper. Once I find my flow, it takes on a form of its own. Sentences become paragraphs and paragraphs become stories. That's literally how this book was born.

God never asks you to do anything He hasn't already equipped you to do. When you lean into God and allow Him to work in you, you'll be surprised what you can do. "For it is God who works in you both to will and to do for His good pleasure." (Philippians 2:13)

Trust God and unleash your power to create.

Affirmation: I am blessed with creativity. Ingenuity and innovation flow through me. My creativity serves a purpose in my life and the world.

Scripture References
Genesis 6:22
Ephesians 2:10
Philippians 2:13
Philippians 3:14

PEARL #21

You Are a Gift!

A spiritual gift is given to each of us so we can help each other.
1 Corinthians 12:7 (NIV)

God has uniquely gifted you with talents and abilities. There is an essential role for you in the body of Christ. Just as there are many parts in our natural body, there are many parts that make up the spiritual body. Every limb in your body has a specific task. If one does not function properly, it causes other parts of the body to malfunction.

There are different kinds of gifts, but the same Spirit distributes them. (1 Corinthians 12:4) Every spiritual gift is essential to the body—no matter how large or small. If everyone was the hand, where would the foot be? And if everyone was an eye, where would the ear be? "But God has set the members, each one of them, in the body just as He pleased. And if they were all one member, where would the body be?" (1 Corinthians 12:18-19)

Your gift is not just for you. It is for someone else. Your gift was given to you to give away. When we all function in our role, it helps the whole body to grow healthy and strong— building itself with love. (Ephesians 4:16) Just imagine how wonderful the world would be if we all embraced this truth.

Affirmation: I am thankful for the gift(s) God placed in me. I will do my part. I will use my gift(s) to be a blessing to others.

Scripture References
1 Corinthians 12:7
1 Corinthians 12:12-14
Ephesians 4:16
James 1:17

PEARL #22

Be Salt

You are the salt of the earth...
Matthew 5:13

*"Not everyone like all our flavors, but each
flavor is someone's favorite."*
Irv Robbins

Have you ever tasted a meal without any flavor? I don't know about you, but I prefer my food to be well-seasoned. I like to marinate some dishes overnight so that they can absorb all the seasonings before it is time to cook them. I discovered the longer it sits, the better the flavor. That's what makes some leftovers taste better than the first day they were prepared.

Although salt makes food very tasty, the actual value of salt is not just in flavoring, but as a preservative. It keeps meats and foods from spoiling by extending their shelf life. In the Old Testament, salt was part of the sacrificial grain offering. (Leviticus 2:13) Ezekiel and the priest also sprinkled salt on the sacrificial burnt offerings unto God. (Ezekiel 43:23) The salt symbolizes purity, preservation, worth, and covenant.

As children of God, you are the salt of the earth. You bring flavor to everything you do. But in addition to bringing flavor, you serve as a preservative to the human race. You are deemed valuable in the earth. You enhance everything in which you come in contact with.

Salt is vital to life. Without it, life would be pretty bland. We have the wonderful privilege of sprinkling our salt with Godly influence so we can preserve the world from moral decay.

But we must be mindful to stay pure, so we don't lose our saltiness or become too salty, we lose our influence in worldly culture. (Matthew 5:13)

Affirmation: I am the salt of the earth. I am a valuable commodity. I bring flavor and life to all that I do.

Scripture References
Leviticus 2:13
Ezekiel 43:23
2 Kings 2:20-22
Matthew 5:13-14
Colossians 4:6

PEARL #23

Shine Bright

You are the light of the world.
Matthew 5:14

"Nothing can dim the light which shines from within."
Maya Angelou

Before God created the earth, it was dark and without form. The first thing He did was speak light, and light came into existence. Then He made a distinction between light and darkness, calling the light day and the darkness night. (Genesis 1:3-5)

In the New Testament, God refers to His children as the light of the world. How profound is it that He guides us to the very first thing He spoke into existence? We were created in His likeness to bring light to a world filled with spiritual darkness.

Light is a source of energy that illuminates and expels darkness. God desires us to shine our lights so that those who walk in darkness will see the marvelous light of Jesus Christ.

Just like a lighthouse emits light to warn mariners of danger or to navigate boats to a safe harbor, we are called to be a light to those who are lost and rescue them from harm. Don't hide your light.
There's nothing little about the light you shine. Stay lit!

Affirmation: I am the light of the world. I shine bright like a diamond. I will not dim my light to please others.

Scripture References
Genesis 1:3-5
Matthew 5:14-16
Luke 8:16
Ephesians 5:13
1 John 1:7

PEARL #24

Hidden Treasure

But we have this treasure in earthen vessels, that the excellence of the power may be of God and not of us.
2 Corinthians 4:7

"Stop looking outside for scraps of pleasure or fulfillment, for validation, security, or love – You have a treasure within that is infinitely greater than anything the world can offer."
Eckhart Tolle

God placed everything in you to accomplish your purpose here on earth. Although it may be laying doormat, it's still on the inside. It is your job to tap in and discover those hidden treasures.

It's incredible the number of talented people who never come into the fullness of their gifts. Dr. Myles Munroe made this somber yet prolific statement,

"The wealthiest place on the planet is just down the road. It is the cemetery. There lie buried companies that were never started, inventions that were never made, bestselling books that were never written, and masterpieces that were never painted. In the cemetery is buried the greatest treasure of untapped potential."

For you are a holy people to the Lord your God, and the Lord has chosen you to be a people for Himself, a special treasure above all the peoples who are on the face of the earth. (Deuteronomy 14:2)

I can see why we are prone to hide our treasures. Perhaps we feel that someone would take them or abuse them. It's like fine China on display but never being used.

Come out of hiding. Don't bury your treasure. The world is waiting for you to present your gifts.

***

Affirmation: I am God's prized possession. I am a precious gem. I am a valuable treasure.

***

Scripture References
Deuteronomy 14:2
Matthew 13:44
2 Corinthians 4:7

PEARL #25

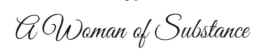

A Woman of Substance

Your eyes saw my substance, being yet unformed.
And in Your book they were written…
Psalm 139:16

"Be not deceived with the first appearance of things,
for show is not substance."
English Proverb

A Teacher did a study observation on her Kindergarten class. She took a few assorted boxes and wrapped them in wrapping paper. Some were wrapped beautifully, and some were not as appealing. Then she asked her students to select a package of their choice. There was no surprise; most of the students chose the beautifully decorated packages. The less appealing ones were left on the table. Each student got a chance to open their box, only for them to discover their box was filled with colorful tissue paper. The teacher finally took one of the not so nicely wrapped boxes and opened it. There was a beautiful gift inside.

You may be familiar with the wise saying, "you can't judge a book by its cover," and I totally agree. How often do you make choices based on the look of a package? Unfortunately, TV, advertisements, music videos, and social media paint a false image of what most of us deem acceptable and unacceptable in our society.

There is so much more to you than your exterior. It is so easy to get caught up in the superficial, such as appearance or material possessions.

The Lord had to remind Samuel of this fact when He was going to anoint the next king. "The Lord does not see as man sees; for man looks at the outward appearance, but the Lord looks at the heart." (1 Samuel 16:7)

You have substance! The world needs women of substance, not just a pretty face with a voluptuous body. Your outer appearance should be a reflection of the inner work that God is doing in you. God desires to work on the inner layers: low self-esteem, insecurities, anger, jealousy, and resentment, so that you are whole and complete.

As a woman of substance, you have power, influence, and great worth.

Affirmation: I am a woman of substance. My strength and values lie within. I am a force to be reckoned with.

Scripture References
1 Samuel 16:7
Psalm 139:16
Proverbs 31:10-31
2 Corinthians 4:7
Colossians 3:12-17
James 1:4

PEARL #26

Complete in Christ

And He said unto her, Daughter,
thy faith hath made thee whole…
Mark 5:34 (KJV)

"The world will never appreciate the wholeness of
who you are as long as you continue to promote the pieces."
Dr. Angela Anderson

Life is filled with peaks and valleys. The issues we face can weigh heavily on us, often leaving us broken and fragmented. This was such the case with the woman with an issue of blood. Her medical condition made her an outcast in society. She had tried many physicians, but her condition didn't get any better. If anything, it got worse. She endured this issue for 12 years! Most of us would have accepted the condition and given up. But this woman didn't.

She heard about Jesus and pressed her way through the crowd. She believed in her heart if she could but touch Jesus' garment she would be made well. (Mark 5:28 KJV) One touch is all it took, and immediately she received her healing. This woman's faith was so infectious that it caught Jesus' attention. Out of all the people surrounding Him, He recognized one specific touch. He stopped to see who touched His clothing. With fear and trembling, the woman came forward and told Him the whole truth. Jesus replied, "Daughter, your faith has made you whole." (v. 34)

To be made whole is to be complete, lacking nothing. From that day on she never had to worry about that infirmity plaguing her again. Although her name was not revealed, her story will never be forgotten. She went from living a life of obscurity to being one of the most faith-featured characters in the Bible.

Affirmation: I am healthy. I am whole. I am complete. I lack nothing.

Scripture References
Matthew 6:22
Matthew 19:26
Mark 5:25-35
James 1:4

PEARL #27

You Are a Masterpiece

*For we are His workmanship, created in
Christ Jesus for good works...*
Ephesians 2:10

*"You are allowed to be both a Masterpiece and a
work in progress, simultaneously."*
Unknown

God is a masterful craftsman. His most pleasurable work was forming man. His raw material was the dust from the ground. He took the dust and masterfully formed and shaped man into His image. Then He breathed into us the breath of life, and man became a living being. (Genesis 2:7)

The woman was His final creation. He saved the best for last. We were formed from the rib of man. After He made woman, He didn't create another thing.

As we surrender to His plan, we will experience the continual unfolding of His purpose in our lives. Like the work of a skilled Potter, God sees what will become *before* we become it.

We are like a piece in a jigsaw puzzle; every piece is essential to the Master's plan. As we remain in His hands, we will find the perfect place where we fit.

You are an amazing work of art. You are God's Masterpiece.

Affirmation: I am a Masterpiece – perfectly designed by my Creator. I am a woman of stature – God's work of art. I am extremely valuable.

Scripture References
Genesis 2:7
Psalm 139:13-14
Ephesians 1:4
Ephesians 2:10
2 Timothy 2:21

PEARL #28

I Am Who God Says I Am

You are a holy people to the Lord your God; the Lord your God has chosen you to be a people for Himself, a special treasure above all the peoples on the face of the earth.
Deuteronomy 7:6

"The more you reaffirm who you are in Christ, the more your behavior will begin to reflect your true identity."
Unknown

We all need a little affirmation every now and then. To affirm is simply to encourage, support, or confirm. The problem is that we often look externally to other people for validation instead of looking to the One who already validated us.

The enemy would like nothing more than for us to lose sight of our true identity. When these moments come, we don't have to look any further than to the Word of God. The Word says, I am fearfully and wonderfully made; I am chosen; I am anointed; I am loved; I am God's prized possession; I am the apple of His eye and I am blessed. There are countless other affirmations in the Bible to encourage you and affirm that you belong to God.

We are a product of our subconscious thoughts. Our thoughts are the result of what we repeatedly think about, which ultimately forms our beliefs. However, we can eradicate any thoughts that do not align with our purpose and replace them with those that speak to who God says we are.

Take a moment to write down any negative beliefs you may have on the left side of a sheet of paper. Then on the opposite side of the paper, write down what God's Word says about you. For example, if you are dealing with fear, place it on the left side of the paper, and on the right side, write, "For God has not given *me* a spirit of fear, but of power and of love and a sound mind." (2 Timothy 1:7) When we declare the Word, we are replacing our truth with God's truth.

After you have completed your list, place it somewhere where you can visibly see it each day. Recite your affirmations every morning as you look in the mirror and allow them to resonate in your spirit. Conclude by saying, "I am who God says I am."

It doesn't matter what others say about you; it's what you say and believe about yourself. Let God's Word be the final say.

Affirmation: I am approved by God. I am who He says I am. That is all the validation I need.

Scripture References
Deuteronomy 7:6
Psalm 17:8
Psalm 139:14
Romans 8:30
2 Corinthians 10:5
Galatians 1:0
2 Timothy 1:7

PEARL #29

Know I'm Not

"Who do men say that I am?"
Mark 8:27

"Don't be confused between what people say you are and who you are."
Oprah Winfrey

Knowing who you are in Christ is just as important as knowing who you are not. I remember when I would get offended by someone calling me something that I knew I was not. Then one day, I had an epiphany. Why in the world would I get offended over something that I knew wasn't true? That thought really liberated me.

It is natural to want to vindicate yourself when someone does not see you for who you are. But life has taught me that people will make an assessment about you no matter how much you try to convince them otherwise. Jesus faced some of these same issues the brief time He walked the earth. We can learn from His approach to the naysayers. He didn't try to convince them of who He was. He just simply said what His Father would say, "I Am Who I Am." He was determined to be about the Father's business.

His purpose was more significant than trying to get people to see who He was. We should also adopt this approach when faced with those who do not understand who we are. Instead of getting bent out of shape or trying to convince people of who you are, simply say, "I am who I am."

Sometimes the best way to silence your naysayers is to keep quiet and keep being. Your value doesn't decrease based on someone's ability not to see your worth. God knows who you are, and that settles it.

Affirmation: I am bold. I am confident. I know who I am, and I know who I'm not.

Scripture References
Exodus 3:14
Matthew 27:14
Luke 22:70
John 14:6

PEARL #30

I Am Loved

"I have loved you with an everlasting love…"
Jeremiah 31:3

There is no greater love than the love of God. He loves us with an everlasting love. His love is unconditional. His love is the purest form there is. He loves us and all our imperfections. We cannot exhaust the love He has for us.

God so loved the world that He gave His only begotten Son, that whoever believes in Him should not perish but have everlasting life. (John 3:16)

It is so great to know that we don't have to earn God's love. We don't have to put on a facade. He loves us just the way we are. He stands with outstretched arms, ready to embrace those who call upon His name.

I'm sure it's hard to fathom a love like this, especially amongst all the hatred we see in the world. But God desires that all His people would have the power to understand how wide, how long, how high, and how deep His love is for us. (Ephesians 3:18 NLT) Although we don't always make the right choices and make mistakes, His love never ceases. Nothing can separate us from the love of God. (Romans 8:38-39) Embrace His love today.

Affirmation: I am loved by God more than I can fully imagine.

Scripture References
Jeremiah 31:3
John 3:16
Romans 8:38-39
Ephesians 3:18
1 John 4:9

PEARL #31

I Am Becoming

And we all…are being transformed into His image.
2 Corinthians 3:18

*"For me, becoming isn't about arriving somewhere or
achieving a certain aim.
I see it instead as forward motion, a means of evolving,
a way to reach continuously toward a better self.
The journey doesn't end."*
Michelle Obama

Our lives are forever evolving. From childhood to adulthood, we learn to transform into the next stage of life. Some things are innate and other things we learn along the way.

When I was a little girl, my god-sister and I played house. We would take the baby dolls and care for them like they were our own. We also enjoyed playing make-believe. Our imaginations would run wild. I didn't realize that a simple thing, like playing make-believe, was developing and shaping me for my future. I understand now that:

> I was a wife long before I became a wife.
> I was a mother long before I became a mother.
> I was a businesswoman long before I became a businesswoman.
> I am wealthy long before I become wealthy.
> I am successful long before I become successful.

What are you on the verge of becoming? The truth is, it is already in you. It's just waiting to manifest.

Never cease becoming.

***

Affirmation: Every day, I am transforming into His image. I am embracing the beauty of simply being and becoming.

***

Scripture References
John 2:11
2 Corinthians 3:18
1 Peter 1:20
1 John 3:2

PEARL #32

The Right Kind of Confidence

Now, this is the confidence that we have in Him, that if we ask anything according to His will, He hears us.
1 John 5:14

"Be so confident in who God called you to be that others want to meet your God to find that same confidence."
Unknown

Life brings many challenges. Yet as you seek God, you will see your challenges as opportunities to learn and grow when you walk in confidence. Confidence is a knowing and assurance that whatever you believe is possible. Jesus operated in confidence on earth. The religious people didn't know how to take Him. He spoke and walked in His Kingdom authority. He knew who He was and didn't shrink back from His assignment. (John 10:18)

As believers, we have the right to exercise that same authority because greater is He in us than in the world. (1 John 4:4)

Do not put your confidence in your flesh. Your confidence is in God. (Philippians 3:3) I like to refer to it as "Godfidence." It's that moment you decide to place your trust in Him to do what you cannot do in your own natural abilities. You strengthen and develop your "Godfidence" through prayer and applying His word into your daily life. Always know that you can do all things through Christ, who gives you strength. (Philippians 4:13)

Affirmation: I put no confidence in my abilities. I walk in Godfidence.

Scripture References
John 10:18
Philippians 3:3
Philippians 4:13
1 John 4:4
1 John 5:14

PEARL #33

The Beauty of Authenticity

He who walks with integrity walks securely,
but he who perverts his ways will become known.
Proverbs 10:9

"Ain't nothing like the real thing."
Marvin Gaye

I am a foodie. My favorite cuisines are Italian and Portuguese. There is something about the flavors that I love. I also enjoy making my own dishes. On various occasions, I have gone to chain restaurants and have not been satisfied. Although the food is tasty, there is no comparison to a truly authentic restaurant specializing in Italian or Portuguese cuisines.

Similarly, we are all incredibly unique and bring our flavor to whatever we do. Even identical twins have distinctive fingerprints. Although we may have similarities, no two people are entirely the same. That's the beauty of authenticity.

Authenticity is being true to oneself, despite the external pressure to conform. The Word tells us not to conform to this world (Romans 12:2), yet we have so many people aspiring to be someone else. Although that may sound flattering, God created us to be original. Why settle to be counterfeit when you can be the real thing? Give yourself permission to live authentically. Dare to be different.

Affirmation: There is only one me, and every day I am afforded the opportunity to show up as my true self. I embrace who I am, and all God has called me to be.

Scripture References
Proverbs 10:9
Luke 12:2
Matthew 5:8
Romans 12:2
2 Corinthians 6:17
1 Peter 2:9

PEARL #34

Imposter Syndrome

And there we saw the giants… We were in our own sight as grasshoppers, and so we were in their sight.
Numbers 13:33

"We don't see things as they are, we see them as we are."
Anais Nin

What do you do when the enemy is the "inner you"? There's an inner critic in us all, whether we choose to admit it or not. If left to fester, our inner thoughts can take an emotional toll on us. Some of these thoughts are self-imposed limitations we have placed on ourselves, while others are limitations people have imposed on us. Whatever the case may be, one thing is for sure: there is an inner struggle that we can't ignore.

Imposter syndrome is real. It stems from guilt or fear of not measuring up. It is extremely common among high-achievers, perfectionists, and people-pleasers. If left unchecked, it can paralyze us from taking action.

In the book of Numbers, we see a very similar case of imposter syndrome. Moses sent twelve men to spy out the land of Canaan. This was the land God had promised that the Israelites would possess. Ten men came back with an unfavorable report. They witnessed the land flowing with milk and honey, but they also saw that the people were strong and powerful. These ten spies saw the people as giants and felt like grasshoppers in their sight.

One of the greatest fights we will ever face is the fight within ourselves. Every promise comes with opposition, and we must overcome the opposition before we can attain the promise. God would not have promised them the land if He knew they were not capable of possessing it.

There were only two spies, Joshua and Caleb, who viewed the situation from a different perspective. They both believed the Israelites were well able to possess the land.

When we are faced with life challenges, we must remind ourselves of God's Word. Instead of focusing on our inadequacies, like the ten spies, we should model the faith of Joshua and Caleb. The mind is where the battle is won.

Affirmation: I am strong and courageous. I possess great power. With God, I am able to conquer anything.

Scripture References
Numbers 13:28-33
Philippians 4:13
1 John 4:4

PEARL #35

Dare to Be Rare

*I will make people scarcer than pure gold,
more rare than the gold of Ophir.*
Isaiah 13:12 (NIV)

"Rare is the union of beauty and purity."
Juvenal

Natural pearls are formed without human intervention. These are pearls in their purest form. They are typically grown within the "wild" living oysters in the sea. Natural pearls are rare and this makes them very valuable.

This is not true of the cultured pearl. These pearls are farm-raised for mass production. The shell of the oyster is slit, and a chemical substance is inserted to produce the pearl. Although the cultured pearl may look like the real thing, it does not hold the value of those formed naturally.

Our world culture is designed for us to fit in, yet God created us to stand out. Before we were even a thought in our parent's minds, God knew us and formed us. He intricately designed us to be one of a kind. You are an oddity. You are different. You are unique. You are in a class all by yourself. There is only one you. That's what makes you rare and valuable.

In the words of Dr. Seuss, "You have to be odd to be number one."

Affirmation: I am rare. My rareness sets me apart. I am a woman of distinction. My worth appreciates in value.

Scripture References
Jeremiah 1:5
Psalm 139:13
James 1:18

PEARL #36

Love Yourself!

You shall love your neighbor as yourself…
Matthew 22:39

"Loving yourself starts with liking yourself, which starts with respecting yourself, which starts with thinking of yourself in positive ways."
Anonymous

Love yourself. You would think this would be something no one had to tell you. Unfortunately, you will be surprised at the countless number of people who don't. All too often, we are looking to social media or others for love and validation. We place so much emphasis on getting others to love us that we neglect to love ourselves. Loving ourselves is a prerequisite to loving others.

What do you like? What makes you happy? What brings you pleasure? Take time to honestly answer these questions. If you struggle with answers to these questions, ask yourself why?

You cannot expect others to love you if you don't love yourself. Nor should you expect others to figure out how you want to be loved. That's too much pressure!

Loving you means you know your worth. You know what you want. You know what you like, and you will not compromise your standards. A woman who loves herself does not base her worth on external compliments. Her emotional bank account is full, and she is mindful of making small deposits as needed. She knows it doesn't matter what others think of her; it's what she thinks of herself.

Take time to focus on loving YOU! Stop trying to please others. Learn what makes you happy. Do things that demonstrate how much you love yourself. Eat like you love yourself. Move like you love yourself. Speak like you love yourself. Act like you love yourself.

In loving yourself, you are teaching others how to love you.

Affirmation: I choose to love myself. I embrace who I am. I am fearfully and wonderfully made.

Scripture References
Psalm 139:14
Proverbs 19:8
Matthew 22:39
Ephesians 5:29

PEARL #37

Guard Your Heart

*Keep your heart with all diligence, for out of it
spring the issues of life.*
Proverbs 4:23

Do you know that your heart is the doorway to your soul? Studies have shown that eight out of ten young adults feel they are not good enough. Your inner thoughts can often make you feel inadequate. If you are going to overcome these negative feelings, you have to do the inner work of guarding your heart.

In a world consumed with beauty, notoriety, and prestige, it is no wonder why we are so hard on ourselves. The interesting thing is the people we are comparing ourselves to also lack in areas of their lives.

You must guard what comes in—allowing only those things that build you up and keep out those that seek to tear you down. Two ways you can guard your heart is by filtering what you watch and listen to. Most corrupt thoughts are subtle, so you have to be careful not to give them any place to reside.

"Keep your heart with all diligence…" Don't allow the influence of others to degrade your opinion of yourself. If something doesn't agree with the Word, dismiss it and move on. We don't have to entertain every thought or accusation that enters our psyche. We can't control what people say, but we can control what we allow to reside in our hearts. (2 Corinthians 10:4-5)

Finally, beloved, whatever things are true, whatever things are honest, whatever things are just, whatever things are pure, whatever things are lovely, whatever things are of good report, if there is any virtue, and if there is any praise, meditate on these things. (Philippians 4:8)

Affirmation: My heart is a wellspring where love, joy, and peace flow.

Scripture References
Psalm 19:14
Psalm 51:10
Proverbs 4:23
Matthew 15:18-20
2 Corinthians 10:4-5
Philippians 4:8

PEARL #38

Created to Love

And now abide faith, hope, love, these three;
but the greatest of these is love.
I Corinthians 13:13

"Love is the fundamental building block of all human relationships.
It will greatly impact our values and morals. Love is the
important ingredient in one's search for meaning."
Gary Chapman

Love is a universal language. It transcends through race, religion, culture, or any other barrier that tries to divide us. However, love cannot be fully expressed without God. It is God in us that enables love to naturally flow from heart to heart and from breast to breast.

Love is essential to our mental, physical, and spiritual well-being. The heart needs love just as our physical body needs air to breathe. When we walk in love, it allows others to see God living in us. It creates compassion, understanding, and community. It's no wonder Paul writes in 1 Corinthians 13:13 that love is the greatest gift.

God created us to love and for love. It is a gift that we have the pleasure to give as well as receive. Love is such a dynamic force. It has the power to lift heavy burdens and to mend broken hearts. There is no one on earth that does not desire to be loved—no matter how negative one may appear or openly deny this fact.

Love is patient, love is kind. It does not envy; it does not boast;
it is not proud. It does not dishonor others; it is not self-seeking;
it is not easily angered; it keeps no record of wrongs.
Love does not delight in evil but rejoices with the truth. It always protects,
always trusts, always hopes, always perseveres.
Love never fails.
1 Corinthians 13:4-8 (NIV)

Affirmation: I am created to love and to be loved. My love is multilingual—it knows no barriers.

Scripture References
John 13:35
Romans 13:8
1 Corinthians 13
1 John 4:17-19
1 Peter 4:8

PEARL #39

Created to Serve

The Son of Man did not come to be served, but to serve...
Matthew 20:28

"He who is greatest among you shall be a servant. That's the new definition of greatness... By giving that definition of greatness, it means that everybody can be great, because everybody can serve."
Dr. Martin Luther King Jr.

The greatest fulfillment you will experience in life is serving something greater than yourself. When I look throughout history, I am amazed at the number of people who devoted their lives to serving others for a greater cause. Countless people gave of their time, talent and treasure—often at the risk of losing their lives. It made me wonder, what motivated them to serve so selflessly? Is there something I could do?

Jesus is the perfect example of such service. He humbled himself in the form of man and became a servant to all. His mission was to save those who were lost and to give His life as a ransom for many. (v. 28) When the mother of the sons of Zebedee approached Him to request if her sons could sit on His left and right side in the Kingdom, His response was, "You don't know what you ask..." (Matthew 20:22) It wasn't long until the other disciples received word. They became indignant with the two brothers.

Jesus used this as a teaching lesson to resolve this dispute. He gathered them together and said, "Whoever wants to be great must become a servant. Whoever wants to be first among you must be your slave. That is what the Son of Man has done: He came to serve, not be served…" (Matthew 20:24-28 MSG)

> *"People don't care how much you know*
> *until they know how much you care."*
> **Theodore Roosevelt**

We are all created to serve. Serving is a selfless act of love. We are not to merely look out for our personal interests, but also for the interests of others. (Philippians 2:4)

Perhaps that's why the former generations had such a passion for serving. They were merely modeling the life Christ modeled for us all.

Affirmation: I am called to serve. I am most fulfilled when I'm serving something greater than myself.

Scripture References
Matthew 20:20-28
Philippians 2:4
1 Peter 4:10-11
Galatians 5:13

PEARL #40

I Am Beautiful

He has made everything beautiful in its time.
Ecclesiastes 3:11

"Beauty comes from within, a beautiful heart creates a beautiful person."
Kenyan Proverb

There is beauty in everything God created. When God sees you, He sees beauty. It is the modern-day culture that has marred our image of how we see ourselves. It's no wonder so many feel inadequate or suffer from low self-esteem.

While man looks at the outer appearance, God looks at the heart. (1 Samuel 16:7) True beauty radiates from the inside out. Inner beauty comes from the confidence in knowing who you are. You are more than a cute face and a sexy figure. Designer clothes, makeup, and accessories do not define you. Adorning the body is secondary to nurturing your inner being. What good is beauty without substance?

This is not to suggest that you neglect to adorn yourselves, but I want to emphasize that you should make nurturing your inner being the main priority. Colossians 3:12-16 teaches us to clothe ourselves with compassion, kindness, humility, gentleness, patience, forgiveness, peace, and love.

Physical beauty is fleeting, but inner beauty lasts a lifetime.

Affirmation: My beauty radiates from the inside out. There's more to me than what you see. I have a beauty that doesn't fade.

Scripture References
1 Samuel 16:7
Proverbs 31:30
Ecclesiastes 3:11
Colossians 3:12-16
1 Peter 3:3-4

PEARL #41

Perfectly Flawed

Not that I have already attained, or am already perfect…
Philippians 3:12

"Imperfections are not inadequacies; they are reminders that we're all in this together."
Brené Brown

God does not require human perfection; if that were the case, we would have no need of Him. I have never met a person who thought they were "perfect" in every aspect of their life. The truth is we are not perfect, but we are continually being perfected. We must embrace all of who we are—flaws and all. God does not wait until we are "perfect" to use us for His glory. We are all a work in progress, and we will continue to be until we leave this earth.

Instead of perfection, God desires a personal relationship, which brings us into perfect oneness with Him. I am so grateful that God loves us despite our imperfections. He told Paul, "My grace is sufficient for you, for My strength is made perfect in weakness." (2 Corinthians 12:9) I pray that brings you some relief and takes the pressure off you trying to have it all together.

But let patience have its perfect work… (James 1:4) We are being perfected day by day. As our relationship develops with Christ, our desires become His desires—to please Him.

It's a beautiful feeling when you know who you are and can embrace all you are—the good, the bad, and the indifferent.

Affirmation: I accept my strengths, my weaknesses, and my flaws. I am a beautiful work in progress.

Scripture References
Psalm 139:14
2 Corinthians 12:9
Philippians 3:12
James 1:4

PEARL #42

That's How I'm Wired

Having then gifts differing according to the grace that is given to us, let us use them…
Romans 12:6

"God made everything the way it is because of what it is supposed to do. "
Dr. Myles Munroe

There are many ways to solve one problem. Just like there are many gifts God has given us. Our unique wiring is our superpower. It allows us to express our creativity and bring our distinct signature to all that we do.

God designed us in such a way that our brains respond to things according to how we are wired. Neurons send signals to the brain; the brain processes them and produces the output. The outcome may vary depending on how a person is wired. That explains why you can communicate the same information to two individuals and get two different interpretations.

Our temperaments can tell us a lot about how we are wired. Are you outgoing, even-tempered, optimistic, or pessimistic? Does the thought of social gatherings fuel you or drain you? Do you see the cup as half-full or half-empty? There are no right or wrong answers to any of these questions. It just helps us to understand ourselves better and hopefully gives us an appreciation for others' unique perspectives. There is beauty in our uniqueness.

Affirmation: I embrace all that I am. I'm not weird, just wired differently.

Scripture References
Psalm 139:13-14
Romans 12:4-13
1 Corinthians 12:4-6
Ephesians 2:20

PEARL #43

What Do You Want?

*So Jesus answered and said to him,
"What do you want Me to do for you?"*
Mark 10:51

*"The difference between what you want
and what you get is what you do."*
Bill Phillips

Bartimaeus was a blind man. He was a beggar and happened to be on the roadside as Jesus, His disciples, and a great multitude were passing by. And when he heard that it was Jesus of Nazareth, he began to cry out and say, "Jesus, Son of David, have mercy on me!" (Mark 10:47) People told him to be quiet, but he cried out all the more.

He managed to get Jesus' attention. Jesus stood still and called for him. (v.49) Bartimaeus rose and came to Jesus. And Jesus asked him, "What do you want Me to do for you?" (Mark 10:51) He replied, "Rabboni, that I may receive my sight." Then Jesus said to him, "Go your way; your faith has made you well." And immediately, he received his sight. (v. 51-52)

What stands out the most about this story is Bartimaeus' tenacity. He knew what he wanted. How many of you would have immediately responded to Jesus if He asked you that same question? I honestly don't know if I would have been able to answer that quickly.

It's not that I don't have a list of things I want. But if Jesus were asking me, I would want to make sure I was asking for something I really needed. I believe Bartimaeus' motives were pure. He wanted to see. And immediately after receiving his sight, he began following Jesus... (v. 52)

How about you? Do you know what you want? If God were to grant your petition, would it draw you closer to Him or from Him? God doesn't have a problem giving us what we want as long as what we want doesn't take the place of Him. Before you answer the question, check your motives.

***

Affirmation: My thoughts and desires are pure. I will let nothing separate me from the love of God.

***

Scripture References
Psalm 37:4
Mark 10:46-52
Mark 11:24
Romans 8:38-39

PEARL #44

What Do You Need?

And my God shall supply all your need according to His riches in glory by Christ Jesus.
Philippians 4:19

"God delights in providing His children with what they need when they rely on Him."
T.D. Jakes

During one of my personal coaching sessions, I had to complete an exercise that required me to list my needs. It was eye-opening to realize how difficult it was to identify my own needs. I probably would have done better solving a math equation without the help of a formula.

Articulating what we need is challenging—especially for most women. We are so used to putting the needs of others before our own; we never take time to consider our needs.

Part of knowing our purpose is discovering our needs. We must settle down long enough to answer those tough questions. Otherwise, we will remain stuck left to repeat vicious cycles.

God is willing and able to supply all we need. But first, we must get clear on what they are. Once that is done, pray and have faith to believe that He will do it.

God knows what we need before we ask, but He wants us to articulate them. Make your request known unto God. It is His good pleasure to give you the kingdom. (Luke 12:32)

Affirmation: I am getting better each day at articulating my needs. I deserve the best, and I want everything that belongs to me.

Scripture References
Psalm 37:4
Philippians 4:19
Mark 11:24
Luke 12:32
1 John 5:15

PEARL #45

Just Ask

Ask, and it will be given to you...
Matthew 7:7

"You get in life what you have the courage to ask for."
Oprah Winfrey

Asking for help has never been my strong suit. I believe it's partially because I am a "Helper." I am usually on the giving end. I'm sure many of you can relate. Like me, if you are a natural giver you often find it very difficult to receive.

My other apprehension is the disappointment I may feel *if* I am denied. Reasoning gets in the way of me asking. What if they say no? What if they are not available? What if? What if? What if? By the time these thoughts are running through my mind, I have talked myself out of asking in the first place.

God is concerned with every detail of our lives—no matter how great or small. He is never exhausted from us asking. In fact, He stands ready to act on our behalf. When we ask with the right motives, it is His desire to give us what we request. Are there sometimes delays? Yes. God knows us—even better than we know ourselves. He knows when we are ready. Yet sometimes, we don't receive because we ask with the wrong motives. (James 4:3)

"Keep on asking, and you will receive what you ask for. Keep on seeking, and you will find. Keep on knocking, and the door will be opened to you. For everyone who asks, receives. Everyone who seeks, finds. And to everyone who knocks, the door will be opened." (Matthew 7:7-8 NLT)

The word *ask* literally means to beg. Your level of desire makes a difference. Some people have to hit rock bottom before they ask for anything. But a pauper is not ashamed to beg and will not hesitate to ask out of his poverty. God blesses those who are poor in spirit and realize their need for Him. (Matthew 5:3 NLT)

So, what are you waiting for? Just ask! The only shot we miss is the one we fail to take. Shoot your shot; you have nothing to lose.

Affirmation: I am bold. I am confident. I have the faith to believe that as I delight myself in God, He will grant me the desires of my heart if I just ask.

Scripture References
Matthew 7:7-8
Luke 12:32
James 4:3
Hebrews 4:16
Hebrews 10:35-38

PEARL #46

Blind Spots

And Elisha prayed, and said, "Lord, I pray, open his eyes that he may see."
2 Kings 6:17

"Everyone has two eyes, but no one has the same view."
Unknown

On this purpose journey, I am learning that I not only need people in my life who think like me, but also people who can give me a fresh perspective. Someone who can see what I can't see. Someone who causes me to think outside the box and stretches me in areas that I need to be stretched.

This was the case with Elisha and his young servant, Gehazi. In 2 Kings 6:8-22, the King of Syria was warring against Israel. Every time the Syrians set up camp, Elisha warned the King of Israel of his plan. When the King of Syria got word that Elisha was sharing his plans with the King of Israel, he requested that Elisha be seized.

The Syrians set up camp at night, surrounding the area where Elisha dwelt. Early the next morning, his servant, Gehazi, saw the army surrounding the city with horses and chariots and exclaimed to Elisha, "What shall we do?" (v.15) Elisha replied, "Do not be afraid, for those who are with us are more than those who are with them." (v. 16) Then he prayed for his eyes to be opened so that he may see. And Gehazi saw the mountain full of horses and chariots of fire all around Elisha.

Elisha was able to see what the King of Israel and his young servant, Gehazi, could not see. We all have blind spots. When we are so close to a thing or too emotionally attached to a situation, it's hard to see the forest from the trees. That's why we need to surround ourselves with wise counsel. They can reveal some things we cannot see. "Where there is no counsel, the people fall; but in the multitude of counselors there is safety." (Proverbs 11:14)

Do you have someone in your life who can see what you can't see? Spiritual leaders and mentors are necessary for personal growth and development. Seek wise counsel and remain teachable.

"When the student is ready, the teacher will appear."
Laozi

Affirmation: I am surrounded by great teachers and wise counsel. I am grateful for a fresh perspective.

Scripture References
2 Kings 6:8-22
Proverbs 11:14
Proverbs 13:20
Mark 10:51-52

PEARL #47

Seek Within

Seek, and you shall find.
Matthew 7:7

"What you seek is seeking you."
Rumi

There's an old expression my parents used when I was growing up. They would say, "If you keep looking for something, you're going to find it." Although I mostly heard it used in a negative context, in a nutshell, they were saying, "Don't go looking for trouble because you are bound to find it."

However, there are times when we seek things such as misplaced items, a new career, or a life-long partner, and it feels as if the heavens are shut up. What do you do? You have to keep seeking. I know this may not be the answer you want to hear, but sometimes it's a matter of you getting in the right place mentally and spiritually before the tangible thing you seek can be found.

"Seek, and you shall find." To seek means to search earnestly. "You will seek Me and find Me when you seek Me with your whole heart." (Jeremiah 29:13) Anything that we will ever need can be found when we learn to seek God first. (Matthew 6:33) When we finally take our minds off the "thing" we are looking for, it will appear.

Patty Labelle's 1977 song, "You Are My Friend," was one of her greatest hits of all time. There was a central message repeated throughout the chorus. It simply says, "I've been looking around, and you were here all the time." Oh, the amazing things we can see if we just learn to seek.

When seeking, it may seem like we will never find what we're looking for, but when we are indeed ready, we'll find that the "thing" we seek is seeking us.

Keep seeking!

Affirmation: All that I seek is already within me.

Scripture References
Jeremiah 29:13
Proverbs 11:27
Matthew 6:33
Matthew 7:7

PEARL #48

Speak & Seek

For everyone who asks receives, and he who seeks finds…
Matthew 7:8

Most people become weary when seeking, as seeking takes time. It requires patience, and we all know that is a lost art in our society. Who has time to wait? Yet, when reading the life of Jesus, nothing in the Bible mentions that He was in a rush.

Just think of all the things we overlook when we are so busy rushing from one place to another. To seek is simply to search for something until you find it. When seeking, you can't be in a rush. Our job is to seek; God's job is to help us find it.

It has always been a running joke with a few of my friends that I will intentionally seek a parking space. I have been doing it for years. Whether at the mall, local grocery store, or work, I position myself in the area where I desire to park and wait for God to show me my spot.

One day a sister-friend and I got together for lunch. When we approached the restaurant, I was reminded how hard it was to find parking in that town. I circled the parking lot and came across the area that I desired to park in and waited. My sister-friend sat on the passenger side and smiled. She knew it was just a matter of time before I got what I wanted. We watched as people began to walk to their cars. In minutes three parking spots became available in the area I was seeking—one of which was right in front of the restaurant. Guess which one I chose? I looked over to my sister-friend, smiled, and said, "That's my Daddy!"

This doesn't just happen with parking spaces. I have seen this work throughout my life whether it's job opportunities, the purchase of my home, vehicles, or choosing my mate, the key is knowing what you want. I love a quote Lynn Richardson shared on a podcast interview; she said, "Speak what you seek until you see what you say.

A persistent seeker finds what they are looking for.

Affirmation: My words and thoughts have power. I only speak those things I want to see manifested in my life.

Scripture References
Matthew 7:8
Proverbs 8:17
Jeremiah 29:13
Hebrews 11:6

PEARL #49

Walk in Truth

You will know the truth, and the truth will set you free.
John 8:32 (NIV)

"This above all, to thine own self be true."
William Shakespeare

There is no greater freedom than when you are walking in truth. But you will be surprised by the number of people who don't choose that route. Whether it's the pressure to blend in with society or the lies we succumb to on social media, we have all found ourselves saying things that do not align with our values and beliefs—just to be part of the "in crowd".

As believers in Christ, we are not to conform to the things of this world. We are to be transformed by renewing our minds so that we may prove what is good, acceptable, and the perfect will of God. (Romans 12:2) Jesus says, "I am the way, the truth and the life." (John 14:6) If the Son sets us free, we are free indeed. (John 8:38)

Walking in your truth takes courage. It means traveling the narrow road. It could sometimes feel lonely. But by choosing freedom, you choose to liberate someone else. Just think of all the trailblazers that have gone before you. They may not have known the difference they were making at the time, but they are now iconic figures who are remembered for their bravery by standing up for what they believed.

Whose life are you called to impact? Do it with all your heart; do it with excellence. You never know who's watching.

Affirmation: I am bold. I am brave. I am free to live my truth.

Scripture Reference
Matthew 7:14
John 8:32-38
John 14:6
Romans 12:2

PEARL #50

Mind Your Business

Pay careful attention to your own work, for then you will get the satisfaction of a job well done, and you won't need to compare yourself to anyone else.
Galatians 6:4 (NLT)

I cannot tell you the amount of time that is wasted looking at what others are doing. As if someone else's life is the barometer by which you should measure your life. There is absolutely nothing wrong with admiring what another person is doing, but it's another thing to become enamored by it. The Bible refers to this as covetousness.

It is possible to get so consumed by what others are doing that we neglect our own assignment. This is unfortunate, as it leaves the people that we are meant to reach untouched. Someone is waiting on your unique gift and abilities, but you are forfeiting that opportunity when you lust after someone else's gift. Not realizing when you do this, you are essentially saying, "God, I don't like how you made me."

What a shame it would be to spend your life pursuing something that could never be yours. Let's live a life to carry out our sole purpose. To live in comparison is to live in defeat.

"Comparison is the most poisonous element in the human heart because it destroys ingenuity and robs peace and joy."
Unknown

Affirmation: I make a conscious decision to mind my business and live the life God designed for me.

Scripture References
Exodus 20:17
Luke 12:15
Galatians 6:4
Hebrews 13:5
James 3:16

PEARL #51

Step by Step

*The steps of a good man are ordered by the Lord,
And He delights in His way.*
Psalm 37:23

"The power to change your life lies in the simplest of steps."
Steve Maraboli

Life is a journey, not a destination. It's easy to become discouraged when pursuing purpose. We may have a mental picture of the outcome, but we have no clue how to start or get there. Our purpose is often revealed to us in glimpses. As we act on what we know, we immediately know more. We accomplish this by taking one step at a time.

In this fast-paced society, we are so used to getting everything in an instant. Life doesn't work that way. There are steps to anything we desire to achieve in life. There is a reason for the steps. We may not always understand it, but trust the process. God knows what He is doing. "Let patience have its perfect work." (James 1:4)

The steps are designed to develop and prepare us to step into what God has for us. God is intentional. He can see what we can't see. As we journey through life, we will discover, it's only by looking back that we can connect the dots. Thank God He doesn't give us what we want before it's time.

It's not necessary to see the entire staircase–just take the next step. Never underestimate the power of your next step.

Affirmation: I'm grateful for each step I take. Every step is necessary for my personal development.

Scripture References
Isaiah 40:29-31
Psalm 37:23
Romans 8:25, 28
Hebrews 12:1-2
James 1:4

PEARL #52

Deeply Rooted

Now he who received seed among the thorns is he who hears the word, and the cares of this world and the deceitfulness of riches choke the word, and he becomes unfruitful.
Matthew 13:22

During the natural growth process, it is imperative that the seed is in the right soil. The right amount of soil allows the seed to germinate. As it continues to grow, it begins to take root. Roots represent stability. They are the fundamental cause, source, and origin of a thing. God is our source. Therefore, as we allow Him to nourish our spirit, our roots grow. The deeper the roots, the stronger we become.

Strong roots thrive when they strike a constant flow of water. Water represents the Word of God. The Word is our nourishment. We must replenish our souls by reading and applying the Word to our lives.

When the storms of life come, it shows us what we are made of. The inner work is necessary to endure this process. The deeper our roots in the Word, the greater our chances of survival.

The sustainability of life is in the root. Stay rooted and grounded in Christ. (Colossians 2:7)

Affirmation: My roots run deep. I am firmly planted and replenished daily by the water of the Word of God.

Scripture References
Isaiah 46:4
Psalm 3:5
Matthew 13:22
John 4:13-14
Colossians 2:6-7
Ephesians 5:26

PEARL #53

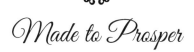

Made to Prosper

*Beloved, I wish above all things thou mayest prosper
and be in health, even as thy soul prospereth.*
3 John 1:2 (KJV)

The word "prosper" is typically associated with material wealth, but God is not only concerned about our finances. God is concerned about our total well-being: mind, body, soul, and spirit. An accumulation of wealth may satisfy you temporarily, but if you aren't making consistent deposits into your spiritual, emotional, and physical bank accounts, it can lead to distress and despair. While you are on the path to financial wellness, let's not become bankrupt in these other areas of your life.

When reconciling your financial bank account, you typically take your monthly statement and cross-reference all transactions to see if the balances are in agreement. If the account does not balance, you will generally go back to determine the issue. Trying to find the error could sometimes be tedious, but when found, it can be quickly resolved.

The same is true with your spiritual bank account. When you are reconciled spiritually, you bring yourself in harmony with God, allowing Him to detect any discrepancies pending your account. "Now all things are of God, who has reconciled us to Himself through Jesus Christ and has given us the ministry of reconciliation…" (2 Corinthians 5:18) Paul implores those who follow Christ to be reconciled to God. (2 Corinthians 5:20)

Your mental and physical well-being are just as important. Your body is a temple, and you maintain it by eating healthy, exercising, and getting the proper rest. When you do these things regularly, you make deposits to your overall well-being, resulting in a balanced life.

Affirmation: I am prosperous. I am rich spiritually, mentally, physically, and financially.

Scripture References
Psalm 1:3
1 Corinthians 6:19-20
2 Corinthians 5:18-20
3 John 1:2

PEARL #54

The Tortoise and The Hare

*Run [your race] in such a way that you may
seize the prize and make it yours!*
1 Corinthians 9:24 (AMP)

The Tortoise and the Hare is a timeless folktale that begins with others poking fun at a slow tortoise. One, in particular, was the hare. The hare was known for his quick speed and was confident that he could outrun the slow tortoise.

The hare challenges the tortoise to a race, and the tortoise reluctantly accepts. The hare thought he had the race in the bag, so he drifted off in the woods and took a nap. The tortoise continued slow and steady on the path and surprisingly began to approach the finish line. The crowd began to cheer. They cheered so loudly the hare woke up. When he noticed the tortoise was in the lead, he immediately kicked into overdrive. Unfortunately, it was too late. The tortoise won the race.

This story is a beautiful illustration of how we should view life's journey—with courage and perseverance. We should not run with uncertainty, but we should run in such a way that we may win the race. (1 Corinthians 9:24) We must keep our eyes on the prize. Life is not a sprint. It's a marathon. Slow and steady wins the race.

*The race is not to the swift, Nor the battle to the strong;
But time and chance happen to them all.*
Ecclesiastes 9:11

The longer I live, the more I discover it doesn't matter who wins the race; it matters who finishes.

Affirmation: I will keep moving forward. As long as I stay the course and do it God's way, I win.

Scripture References
Ecclesiastes 9:11
Mark 9:35
1 Corinthians 9:24
Hebrews 12:1

PEARL #55

What's the Rush?

Be anxious for nothing, but in everything by prayer and supplication, with thanksgiving, let your requests be made known to God...
Philippians 4:6

It is human nature to want to know something before its time. The suspense could often put us in a state of anxiousness. Our minds start racing a mile a minute. We work ourselves up and immediately think of the worst possible scenario. If we're not careful, these thoughts could quickly spiral us down an unwanted path.

Anxious thoughts are an insult to God. It reveals our lack of trust in Him. We spend our time worrying when we can be enjoying the moment. Worry cannot add a single moment to our lives. (Matthew 6:27) So what's the point of doing it?

When anxious thoughts occur, take time to examine your heart. Be still; quiet your mind, and breathe. Cast your worries and state your concerns to God in prayer. (1 Peter 5:7) Remind yourself that He is in control.

Don't let the worry of the future rob you of the joy of today. Trust in the Lord and allow Him to direct your path.

Affirmation: I choose to walk in peace and find joy in living in the moment.

Scripture References
Proverbs 3:5-6
Matthew 6:25-34
Philippians 4:6
1 Peter 5:7

PEARL #56

Women of Influence

A wise woman builds her home, but a foolish woman tears it down with her own hands.
Proverbs 14:1 (NLT)

"If you educate a man, you educate an individual, but if you educate a woman, you educate a nation."
African Proverb

God gave both man and woman authority to take dominion over the earth. However, our roles are uniquely different. Man's power is his position, and a woman's power is her influence. In Genesis 3, Eve demonstrated her power in the Garden. The serpent deceived her into eating the fruit from the forbidden tree. She also convinced her husband, Adam, to do the same, which ultimately resulted in the fall of man.

There are several examples of women in the Bible who exercised their power of influence –Sarai, Miriam, Rebecca, Jezebel, Esther, and Deborah, just to name a few. These women were influential in their own right. Although some of these women had good intentions, some of their decisions were not godly.

Sometimes influence can be packaged in manipulation or witchcraft. Beware of using your influence for evil. When you know to do good, do it. "For it is better, if it is the will of God, to suffer for doing good, than for doing evil." (1 Peter 3:17)

> *"The power of authentic femininity opens the world to a vast array of different forms of womanhood; each powerfully demonstrative in its own rite."*
> **Wynell Freeman**

God entrusted the woman with a powerful gift, one that must be used with discretion. The power of influence is perfectly demonstrated when we align with the will of God.

Affirmation: I am a woman of influence. I am a force to be reckoned with.

Scripture References
Genesis 3:6
Proverbs 31:12
2 Timothy 1:5
1 Peter 3:1-6
1 Peter 3:17

PEARL #57

I'm Different

*Do not be conformed to this world, but be transformed
by the renewal of your mind...*
Romans 12:2 (ESV)

"In order to be irreplaceable, one must always be different."
Coco Chanel

As children, we played games like "Follow the Leader" and "Simon Says." In essence, we were being taught to mirror what we saw. The more I reflect on it, the more I see why we have such a difficult time coming into our individuality. Culture has a subtle way of conditioning our way of thinking.

The older I have become I have learned to embrace my differences. But this was no easy task. I had to get rid of some subconscious beliefs and be open to learning new things and work to unlearn other things. Curiosity starts with questions. It was then that I became very interested in discovering who I really was. I accepted that I didn't have to be like everyone else. I didn't have to try to fit in. Instead, I could be who God called me to be.

When Jesus stepped on the scene, the Pharisees and Sadducees all had opinions of who He should or shouldn't be. But Jesus didn't waste time trying to explain who He was. He didn't come to blend in with the religious leaders of His day. He was different. He was in a class all by

Himself. He was called to be set apart. His assignment was to transform lives, not conform to the ways of this world.

Think about how much time and energy we waste trying to be liked by people who aren't even happy with themselves. When we choose to be like someone else, we miss out on God's best for us.

God doesn't make carbon copies. No two fingerprints are exactly the same. We were born to be different. It's our differences that make us unique. Dare to be rare.

***

Affirmation: I embrace who I am. I am proud to be me. My uniqueness is my superpower.

***

Scripture References
Matthew 22:41-46
Romans 12:2
2 Corinthians 6:17
1 Peter 2:9

PEARL #58

Shall We Dance?

For in Him we live and move and have our being.
Acts 17:28

"The moment in between what you once were, and who you are now becoming, is where the dance of life really takes place."
Barbara De Angelis

Everything God created has a rhythm. Time has a rhythm. The sun and the earth have a rhythm. The ocean has a rhythm, and every organ in our bodies has a rhythm. Just like the beautiful music of a grand orchestra, life is a beautiful dance choreographed by God. When we place our will in His hands, we set rhythm into motion. He begins to take us on an amazing journey. It's not necessary for us to know the way as long as we allow Him to lead.

God guides us in such a way that requires our complete surrender. Each move is seamless, and every step, dip, and pivot is intentional. It is a reminder that His ways are higher than our ways and His thoughts are higher than our thoughts (Isaiah 55:9).

Here's when most of us veer off track. We try to reason with ourselves or figure out what the next move will be instead of leaning in and leaving the direction up to Him.

Get in tune with God. Allow Him to order your steps, and you will discover life with Him is an amazing symphony.

Affirmation: I embrace the rhythm of life. My mind, body, soul, and spirit are in perfect harmony with God's plan.

Scripture References
Psalm 8:3-4
Psalm 19:1
Psalm 34:1
Psalm 117
Psalm 150:6
Isaiah 55:9
Acts 17:28

PEARL #59

Go with the Flow

*He who believes in Me… out of his heart
will flow rivers of living water.*
John 7:38

A river is a stream of natural water that flows down from the mountains. As the water travels from higher elevations to lower elevations, it is being purified. These rivers are a source of provision for humans, animals, and all living species. There is beauty watching how the water currents flow in perfect harmony. Just as there is constant motion in the water cycle, God has designed our lives to function in the same manner.

As we allow the water of God's Word to flow in our lives, we will experience the continual movement of God in our daily quest. All that is required is an open heart and an open mind. When we stay open to learning and align ourselves with the plan of God, rivers of living water will flow through us.

> "The river of the Spirit of God overcomes all obstacles. Never focus your eyes on the obstacle or the difficulty. The obstacle will be a matter of total indifference to the river that will flow steadily through you if you will simply remember to stay focused on the Source."
> **Oswald Chambers**

There is a rhythm that God set in motion when He made all of creation. Don't exhaust energy swimming against the current. Relinquish control and go with the flow.

Affirmation: I have a river of life flowing through me. I am aligned and in tune with the flow.

Scripture References
Genesis 2:10-14
Deuteronomy 8:6-7
John 7:38
Acts 17:28

PEARL #60

Times of Refreshing – Self-Care

He restores my soul… My cup runs over…
Psalm 23 (NKJV)

*"Begin each day giving yourself to you
before giving yourself away."*
Mikki Taylor

As women, we tend to juggle so many hats, and our energy is diverted to meet the needs of everyone but ourselves. Since we are constantly being drawn from, we must keep our cups full. What good is a well if the well runs dry? God desires that we have a well that continues to spring forth like a river. When we take the necessary action to recharge, refuel and replenish, there is a constant flow of limitless resources.

Matthew 5:6 states, "He that hunger and thirst for righteousness shall be filled." God is our reservoir. He is living water. His fountain never runs dry. When we drink of His water, we will never thirst. (John 4:14) The reservoir is for us; the overflow is for others. Keep your cup full and serve from your saucer.

Just like the rain comes to replenish the earth, God's Word replenishes our Spirit. (Isaiah 55:10) It's essential that we set aside time for refreshing. Be mindful of when you are running low and purposely schedule times to refill. Be intentional in blocking your calendar for rest and quiet time. That may require setting boundaries around people and things that consume your time and energy. Spending time with Jesus is time well spent.

Affirmation: I have a reservoir of living water residing in me. I will set times to tap in and be refreshed.

Scripture References
Psalm 23
Isaiah 55:10
Matthew 5:6
John 4:10-15

PEARL #61

Time of Refueling - Self-Care (2)

*Come to Me, all you who labor and are heavy laden,
and I will give you rest.*
Matthew 11:28

"Take time to refuel. You can't run on empty."
Doreen Ellis

A good mechanic once told me, "to ensure your car runs properly, at minimum, you must get the necessary oil changes." This normally takes place at least every few months or after your vehicle reaches a certain amount of mileage.

We also must ensure to get the proper maintenance needed for our natural bodies. If not, we may find ourselves on the side of the road, in need of major repair.

"Come to Me." God invites us to come to Him. The overworked, the burned out, and the fatigued. It is essential that we discern when to take time to recharge. Contrary to those always on their grind, the body needs at least 7 to 10 hours of rest each day. When we rest, the body gets a chance to restore energy and allow us to function at an optimal level.

God provides the best rest. As we take time to get away with Him, we learn how to live freely and lightly.

Oswald Chambers states, "The measure of the worth of our public activity for God is the private profound communion we have with Him….

We have to pitch our tents where we shall always have quiet times with God, however noisy our times with the world may be."

Our body is our vehicle here on earth. We only get one. If we want to keep it functioning properly, we must take time to fine-tune and unwind. Self-care is not an option; it's a necessity.

Affirmation: I make self-care a priority. It is essential to my well-being.

Scripture References
Exodus 33:14
Exodus 34:21
Matthew 11:28-30
Mark 2:27
Mark 6:31-32

PEARL #62

Preparation Is Key

*Let us be glad and rejoice and give Him glory,
for the marriage of the Lamb has come,
and His wife has made herself ready.*
Revelation 19:7

"By failing to prepare, you are preparing to fail."
Benjamin Franklin

Throughout the Bible, countless stories teach us about the importance of being ready and staying ready. In fact, preparation is the prerequisite to God's promises being fulfilled on the earth. Noah spent decades preparing to build an ark in a land that showed no sign of rain. Moses spent forty years on the backside of a desert before He was called to lead the children of Israel into the Promised Land. Jesus spent thirty years in preparation for a three-year ministry.

Each of these leaders was prepared to carry out God's assignment. They spent time with Him. They sought His guidance, and they obeyed His voice. Although the promise was not fulfilled immediately, they remained faithful and were found ready when it was time to execute.

Preparation takes time, and it is needed for our growth and development. What is God preparing for you?

We are continually evolving. One stage in life is preparing us for the next. It is important that we stay spiritually aligned with God (our Source of Life) to be found ready when the right opportunity comes.

Affirmation: I am in preparation and being made ready for my next assignment.

Scripture References
Genesis 6:13-22
Exodus 3:7-14
Proverbs 6:6-8
Luke 3:23
Revelations 19:7

PEARL #63

Perfection is a Myth

My grace is sufficient for you, for My strength is made perfect in weakness.
2 Corinthians 12:9

"Perfection is a myth and the enemy of productivity."
Unknown

I used to harp on having everything perfect. I'm ashamed to admit the number of opportunities I missed trying to wait for everything to come together just as I imagined. The truth is perfection robs us of making progress. It is a limited mindset.

If you ask anyone who has reached any level of success, they will tell you the best lessons they have learned are from making mistakes. If we desire to grow, we must get comfortable with making mistakes.

Do you suffer from perfectionism? You are not alone. Paul was given a thorn in his flesh so that he did not become too arrogant. He pleaded with God three times to relieve him, but His response was, "My grace is sufficient for you, for my strength is made perfect in weakness." (2 Corinthians 12:9) Paul chose to boast in his imperfection so that the power of God can rest on him.

God uses our imperfections to strengthen us. Give yourself permission to do your best and allow room for improvement. It's about progress, not perfection.

Keep moving forward, trusting that God will perfect those things that concern you. (Psalm 138:8)

Affirmation: It's OK if I make mistakes. Each mistake is an opportunity for me to learn and grow.

Scripture References
Psalm 138:8
2 Corinthians 12:9
Philippians 3:12

PEARL #64

I Am Worth It

Who can find a virtuous woman? For her price is far above rubies.
Proverbs 31:10

"Your value doesn't decrease based on someone's inability to see your worth."
Unknown

A woman of purpose knows her worth. She puts God first and draws her strength and wisdom from Him. Her unique talent and intelligence are a rare commodity. She carries herself with class. She's a woman of distinction. She knows what she wants and will not settle for anything less. Her virtue appreciates in value. She's like a fine wine that gets better with time.

A woman of worth has integrity publicly and privately. Her persona commands respect, but more importantly, she respects herself and others. She's a woman of influence with a great attitude. She brings value to her family, friends, and community. People take notice and call her blessed. Her presence is undeniable, and she makes every effort to live a life of excellence.

Who can find a virtuous woman? For her price is far above rubies.
Proverbs 31:10

You are that woman. God placed all these virtues within you. Know your worth. Don't ask for it. Walk it. Live it. State it and never accept anything less. You are worth it!

Affirmation: I am not a one in a million kind of girl. I am a once-in-a-lifetime kind of woman. I am of infinite value. God made me that way.

Scripture Reference
Psalm 138:13-14
Proverbs 10:9
Proverbs 20:7
Proverbs 31:10-31
Luke 12:6-7

PEARL #65

The Unknown

He went out, not knowing where he was going.
Hebrews 11:8

"Faith never knows where it is being led, but it loves and knows the One Who is leading."
Oswald Chambers

Abraham was a man of great faith. When he was called to go to a place that God would show him, he obeyed and went, not knowing where he was going. Abraham fully trusted God, and it was accounted unto him as righteousness. (Romans 4:3)

Walking in purpose requires faith. We will not know all the details. It requires full allegiance to God. We have to trust His guidance.

Trust in the Lord with all your heart, And lean not on your own understanding; In all your ways acknowledge Him, And He shall direct your paths.
Proverbs 3:5-6

Here is where many believers miss it. We're okay as long as we are familiar with the route. But the problem with that is, sometimes we venture out ahead of Him, only to discover that's not the path He wants us to take. Beware of thinking you know the way. God's way is beyond our comprehension. We must allow Him to navigate our course and trust that He will get us to the assigned destination.

Think about how advanced technology is today. We can now get in our car, enter a destination, and allow a navigational system to tell us where to go. If we take a wrong turn, the navigational system will reroute and put us back on course.

That's how it is when we trust and obey God. He guides us along our path to purpose. If we get off course, we don't have to worry as He is sure to reroute us and get us back on track. When we allow the Spirit to guide us, we don't need to know the way; we can trust the one who does.

God is wiser than any GPS. He is the way, the truth, and the life. (John 14:6) We are never lost as long as He has the wheel.

***

Affirmation: I will trust the Lord and allow Him to direct my path. I am confident in His navigation.

***

Scripture References
Genesis 12:1
Proverbs 3:5-6
Hebrews 11:8
John 14:6
Romans 4:3
Romans 8:14

PEARL #66

The Grace to Forgive

If we confess our sins, He is faithful and just to forgive us our sins and cleanse us from all unrighteousness.
1 John 1:9

"Forgiveness is not a one-time thing that happened the day you received Christ. It is an everyday thing, for the rest of your life."
Joyce Meyer

I believe we have all experienced some type of hurt one time or another. I would also venture to say that we have been guilty of causing someone emotional discomfort or pain—whether intentionally or unintentionally. The truth is, we are human, and we are bound to be on either side of the spectrum as we journey through life.

The question becomes, how do we deal with it? Peter was curious as well, and he asked Jesus, "Lord, how often shall my brother sin against me, and I forgive him? Up to seven times?" Jesus replied, "I do not say to you, up to seven times, but up to seventy times seven." (Matthew 18:21-22)

This tells me that Jesus knew the tendencies of our human nature. He knew we would not always get it right. Yet He tells us if we confess our sins, He is faithful and just to forgive us of our sins and cleanse us from all unrighteousness. (1 John 1:9)

Each year the U.S. Article II of the United States Constitution gives the President the power to pardon citizens of a federal crime. Not only is the person forgiven of the crime, they are excused from any punishment associated with that offense.

When was the last time you forgave someone that may have been guilty for what they have done? Some debts are too great to repay. We must forgive others if we want Christ to forgive us.

Affirmation: I am thankful for God's grace toward me. I, in turn, will show grace toward myself and others.

Scripture References
Matthew 6:14-15
Matthew 18:21-22
Ephesians 1:7
1 John 1:9

PEARL #67

Let it Go!

Forgetting those things which are behind and reaching forward to those things which are ahead…
Philippians 3:13

"We must let go of the life we have planned, so as to accept the one that is waiting for us."
Joseph Campbell

Pursuing purpose requires laser focus. It is the ability to hone in on the desired goal, allowing nothing to divert your attention. For this to take place, we have to learn to let go of some things. It is impossible to embrace what is before us if we keep looking backward. We have to let go of past hurts, past failures, and past mindsets.

Holding on to things prevents us from moving forward. When we choose not to forgive or let go of unpleasant events, we send signals to our subconscious, causing us to see, think or behave irrationally. These thoughts lead to anger, strife, and resentment. The flesh begins to dominate, and our hearts become bitter. This emotional baggage is not healthy. And if it goes unchecked, it can affect us mentally, physically, and spiritually.

As you know, letting go of unforgiveness is for you, not the individual. When we forgive others, Christ forgives us. (Matthew 6:14) It does not mean we forget; it simply means we choose not to let the offense rob us of our joy and peace.

We also need to learn to forgive ourselves. Some may find this more difficult than forgiving others. We tend to hold ourselves to a higher standard – especially those of us who suffer from perfectionism. We must give ourselves the grace to make mistakes.

To embrace the new, we have to leave some things (i.e., old thinking patterns, self-limiting beliefs, toxic relationships, etc.) behind. Keep your eyes on Jesus. Focus on the promise, not the problem, and never lose sight of the goal.

When we let it go, we let our e-go.

Affirmation: I forgive myself and others. I let go of what no longer serves me. I choose to move forward. I choose to be free.

Scripture References
John 8:36
Ephesians 4:31
Philippians 3:13
Hebrews 12:1-2

PEARL #68

To Know Him

That I may know Him and the power of His resurrection, and the fellowship of His sufferings…
Philippians 3:10

Paul was a man rich in knowledge and religious background. He was an earnest searcher of truth and well acquainted with the law. His prestigious pedigree brought him honor and privilege. But all of that changed after his encounter with Christ. His life was completely transformed. He realized those things were worthless in comparison to the spiritual wealth he experienced in Christ. He was willing to lose it all so that he may know Him more. (Philippians 3:7)

We see that Paul pursued God with everything within him. He went from persecuting the church to becoming an advocate for Christ. His fire and zeal were relentless. He found his true purpose. He dedicated the rest of his life to apprehending the One who had apprehended him.

Paul's amazing discovery is one we should all desire. When we truly desire to know Him, we truly begin to know ourselves. God has a plan for every one of us, but we need Him in order to carry it out.

God is working in us to reach His highest goals until His purpose and our purpose become one."
Oswald Chambers

What are you willing to count as a loss to gain a deeper and personal relationship with Christ?

Affirmation: Each day, I am afforded the opportunity to know God more.

Scripture References
Psalm 16:11
Matthew 10:39
Acts 2:28
Philippians 3:7-10

PEARL #69

The Right Attitude

*Let this same attitude and purpose and [humble]
mind be in you which was in Christ Jesus...*
Philippians 2:5 (AMPC)

*"Attitude is the reflection of a person,
and our world mirrors our attitude."*
Earl Nightingale

Attitude is a mere reflection of our mind, will, and emotions. Our attitude shapes the way we view the world and how the world views us. We have the power to change our environment. Positive people naturally attract positive people, just as negative people naturally attract negative people. There's an old proverb that states, "Birds of a feather flock together." In essence, we are what we attract.

If you don't like your current environment, you have the power to change it. It starts with making the necessary attitude adjustments. The right attitude begins with the right self-image. How do you see yourself? The answer to this question will determine how others see you.

Having the right attitude causes people to respond in your favor. Learn to see the good in everything. When you focus on the good, more good comes to you. Rid yourself of negative thinking. Instead, think on those things that are true, honest, just, pure, lovely, and of good report (Philippians 4:8). Keep these thoughts in the center of your mind.

You are a sum total of the thoughts you think. The right attitude is everything.

> *"Your attitude determines your altitude.*
> *Your disposition determines your destiny."*
> **Zig Ziglar**

Affirmation: I maintain a positive attitude at all times. My attitude is contagious. I radiate confidence and well-being. I am what I attract.

Scripture References
Psalm 100:4
Philippians 2:5
Philippians 4:8
1 Timothy 6:6

PEARL #70

Take Time to Unplug

*Come to Me, all you who labor and are
heavy laden, and I will give you rest.*
Matthew 11:28

*"Almost everything will work again if you
unplug it for a few minutes, including you."*
Anne Lamot

As I was logging on to my computer to start my daily routine, I received a notice alerting me that my computer was being updated and I would need to reboot to ensure the refresh took place.

I felt myself getting furious as I was all set to work on my "to do" list, and now I was interrupted with a system update. As I hit the button to accept the notice to restart my computer, I learned a valuable lesson. If a computer system has to reboot and refresh, why don't I take time to pause and allow my internal system to reboot?

In this world of vast technology, we have lost the sensibility to unplug. We wake up to our mobile devices, televisions, and computers. Our minds are immediately flooded with information that we may or may not need. We rely on technology so much that we feel lost without it.

Artificial intelligence has replaced our ability to process. We have so many things tugging for our attention (i.e., emails, text messages, DMs, phone calls, and social media), it's a wonder we can get anything done. Even as I was typing this Pearl, my computer alerted me that the power was running low. Yet another interruption. Technology needs time to recharge, and so do we!

We must master our technology, or our technology will master us. We must take time to unplug and bring our lives into alignment with the true essence of our being—our soul's purpose.

Technology in proper relation brings support and harmony to our lives. It was created to assist us, not rule us. Remember who holds the power.

Affirmation: I will take time to unplug and give my body the proper rest it needs to *rest*ore.

Scripture References
Genesis 2:2-3
Exodus 33:14
Matthew 11:28-29
Mark 6:31

PEARL #71

The Art of Stillness

Be still, and know that I am God…
Psalm 46:10

"The earth has music for those who listen."
William Shakespeare

A few years ago, I visited the chiropractor's office for physical therapy. As I laid on the table, I experienced an unforgettable stillness. My mind was free from random thoughts and the cares of life. I was able to hear myself breathe! Ahh… It was such an amazing yet unusual experience that I wanted to enjoy every minute of it.

I often hear people talk about meditation and yoga but never connected them to the art of stillness. Now I see the benefits of it. The brain is a small fragile organ in our body which is our central processing system. "It controls most of the activities of the body, processing, integrating, and coordinating the information it receives from the sense organs, and making decisions as to the instructions sent to the rest of the body." [1]

Mental and physical health go hand and hand. When you take time to relax and rest, you replenish and refuel your mind. It sounds simple, but it's not so easy to put into practice.

If you shift the letters in the word listen, you will find the word silent. It is so important that we take time for moments of silence. Being still allows your mind to declutter so you can be more decisive and less reactive

---

1 Wikipedia

to things that are going on around you. Schedule times of restoration and take time to listen! A well-rested body heals itself.

Affirmation: I will exercise times of quietness and practice the art of hearing from God.

Scripture References
Exodus 14:13-14 (ESV)
Isaiah 26:3
Psalm 23:1-3
Psalm 46:10
Mark 4:39

PEARL #72

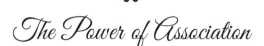

The Power of Association

Do not be deceived: "Evil company corrupts good habits."
1 Corinthians 15:33

"Sometimes your circle decreases in size, but increases in value."
Dolce Ruby

The old wise saying, "Show me your friends, and I'll show you your future," still holds true today.

You can't be around a person for long without them having an effect on you. You are the sum total of the company you keep. The Bible says, "He who walks with wise men will be wise, but the companion of fools will be destroyed." (Proverbs 13:20)

Choose friends that are going in the direction you desire to go. There may be some behind you, some alongside you, and some further ahead of you. The key is that they all are moving forward.

Take a moment to assess your current circle. If you are the smartest one in your circle, your circle is too small.

Below are six valuable lessons I've learned along my journey on relationships.

1. The first relationship we must ensure is intact is our personal relationship with God. He desires a relationship with us, but He will not impose His will on us. As we work on developing our

vertical relationship, He will guide and help us build horizontal relationships. (John 15:1-4, 14-16)
2. Healthy relationships should not be one-sided. Healthy relationships are reciprocal. You want relationships that add and multiply, not subtract and divide. (Proverbs 27:17)
3. Reassess relationships that leave you depleted. These are the people who drain your energy. If this person always makes withdrawals and never makes deposits, it may be time to cut your losses. (Mark 12:12-14, 20-21)
4. Rid yourself of negative people and busybodies. Misery loves company. (1 Corinthians 15:33)
5. You must be willing to lose some relationships to gain the right ones. (Matthew 19:29)
6. Don't give people the liberty to place themselves wherever they want to be in your life. Lovingly put them in their place. Jesus perfectly modeled this on earth. He made many disciples, but He chose the twelve and at times only selected three.

You own the right to be selective. Choose your circle wisely.

Affirmation: I choose friends that add value. I also bring value to my relationships.

Scripture References
Proverbs 27:27
Matthew 19:29
Mark 12:12-14, 20-21
John 15:1-4, 14-16
1 Corinthians 15:33

PEARL #73

Find Your Tribe

He went up on the mountain and called to Him those He Himself wanted. And they came to Him. Then He appointed twelve, that they might be with Him...
Mark 3:13-14 (NKJV)

"Your vibe attracts your tribe."
Unknown

A famous African proverb says, "If you want to go fast, go alone. If you want to go far, go together." No man is an island unto himself. God made us for interdependence. We were created for community.

Even Jesus had a tribe. After a night of prayer on a mountain, He hand-selected twelve disciples from His followers. They were a diverse bunch of various professions and backgrounds. This began the launch of His ministry. There's no question that Jesus could have accomplished His goal alone, but He chose a tribe to fulfill His purpose. As a result, His disciples were able to spread the good news across the world.

We are all designed for fellowship. You are the unique piece to someone's puzzle. You are the solution to someone's dilemma. When you find your tribe, you find your vibe. You feel a sense of belonging. There is a synergy that you can't explain. It allows you to thrive. Things that took days, months, or even years to accomplish, will come together exponentially. The right connections can save you time, energy, and heartache.

The journey is so much sweeter when you are working together to fulfill your purpose.

Affirmation: I am essential to my tribe. I support them, and they support me.

Scripture References
Proverbs 27:17
Mark 3:13-14
Galatians 6:2
1 Thessalonians 5:11
Hebrews 10:24-25

PEARL #74

Remember Who You Are

*Greater is He that is in you, than he
that is in the world.*
1 John 4:4

"When you learn, teach; when you get, give."
Maya Angelou

I love the storyline of the classic Disney movie, "The Lion King." My favorite part is when Simba was faced with opposition and saw his father in a vision. He heard the resounding voice of his father say, "Simba, remember who you are."

Simba's father, Mufasa, had taken time to impart wisdom to his son. He knew that he would not be around forever, and he was grooming his son for kingship. He taught him a valuable lesson about the circle of life. Mufasa was wise and knew the importance of raising a successor.

Who are you training to reign? Who are you pouring into? Are you living to leave a legacy? What will you be known for after you are gone?

Jesus wonderfully demonstrated this with His disciples. After walking, talking, and teaching them, He began to tell them about His transition. He told them, "Very truly I tell you, whoever believes in me will do the works I have been doing, and they will do even greater things than these because I am going to the Father." (John 14:12 NIV) He assured them that they would have a Helper, who will abide in them and guide them in truth. (v.16) Jesus spent quality time equipping his disciples and sharing with them the things to come prior to His departure. (v. 29)

A great leader can see the greatness in others. They have the ability to draw the best out of people and allow them to see what lies within them. They help to cultivate the gift so that they can reach their highest potential. As we learn, we have an obligation to teach. That is mentorship at its finest.

Affirmation: I am called to make an indelible impact on the earth. I will make a difference by imparting wisdom to the next generation.

Scripture References
Psalm 78:1-7
John 14:12
2 Timothy 1:5
1 John 4:4

PEARL #75

Knowing When to Serve or Be Served

Mary has chosen that good part, which will not be taken away from her.
Luke 10:42

"God is far more interested in why you serve others than he is interested in how well you serve them. He's always looking at your heart."
Rick Warren

I am sure Martha had good intentions when she was busy preparing a big dinner for Jesus. It is no question that she had the gift of hospitality. On the other hand, her sister, Mary, chose to sit at Jesus' feet and talk with Him. While Martha was serving, Mary was worshipping. This bothered Martha, so she said to Jesus, "Lord, doesn't it seem unfair to you that my sister just sits here while I do all the work? Tell her to come and help me." (Luke 10:40)

Is it possible that we are too busy trying to serve God that we miss the opportunity to worship Him? Martha didn't take time to assess Jesus' preferences. She just assumed that she should serve. Be careful that you are not busy serving when you should be sitting at the feet of Jesus—being served.

There are so many things tugging for our attention that we can easily get distracted. We must be mindful of seeking God as to what He would have us to do. Our ultimate assignment is to please Him. To do that, we must seek Him first. (Matthew 6:33)

Affirmation: I am honored to serve and be served, and I am thankful for the wisdom to know the difference.

Scripture References
Matthew 6:33
Matthew 25:37-40
Luke 10:38-42

PEARL #76

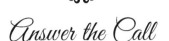

Answer the Call

I heard the voice of the Lord, saying: "Whom shall I send, and who will go for us?" Then I said, "Here am I; Send me."
Isaiah 6:8

"There is no greater gift you can give or receive than to honor your calling. It's why you were born. And how you become most truly alive."
Oprah Winfrey

Have you ever stopped to think, "Why am I here?" There is a purpose for your existence. You are not here just to take up space. God was very intentional on where, when, and why He placed you here on this earth. You are here for a reason, and it is your job to seek Him to receive instruction on how to carry out your assignment.

Your assignment is tailor-made for you. That means you don't have to compete with anyone else because God had you in mind when He created you. You are the right one for the job. And what God has for you is for YOU. No one can stop it; receive it, or take it away.

All that's required is an answer to the call. God will not impose His purpose on your life. He gave you free will. But the moment you do, He will begin to reveal the plans He has for your life.

You were created specifically to be an answer to someone's dilemma. Who's waiting for you to come into your calling? Will you answer the call? Someone's waiting on your yes.

Affirmation: I am a solution to someone's problem. I am committed to showing up and completing the work God has begun in me.

Scripture References
Romans 8:18-19
Isaiah 6:8
Isaiah 54:17

PEARL #77

The Right Balance

Beloved, I pray that you may prosper in all things and be in health, just as your soul prospers.
3 John 1:2

"Balance is the key to everything. What we do, think, say, eat, feel, they all require awareness, and through this awareness, we can grow."
Koi Fresco

When pursuing purpose, it is important that we stay well-rounded. Too much focus in one area can cause a deficiency in another. That is why we often witness people's public success resulting in private failure. God desires us to be fully developed so that we are not lacking in any area of our lives. To do so, we must give attention to these major areas: Mind, Body, Soul, and Spirit.

We are spirit, have a soul, and live in a body. The spirit is the divine nature that gives us purpose and meaning for life. It enables us to love God, ourselves, and others. It also gives us intuition between right and wrong. Our spiritual health plays a significant role in our emotional health, which influences our physical health. The Apostle John wrote in 3 John 1:2, "Beloved, I pray that you may prosper in all things and be in health, just as your soul prospers."

The soul is comprised of our mind, will, and emotions. It is what gives us our personality and how we live out our relationship with God.

It is where our thoughts, beliefs, and attitudes are formed, and our feelings, emotions, and memories are retained. The mind is in constant communication with the body. Whatever our mind thinks, perceives, and experiences send signals from the brain to our bodies. So we must renew our minds daily and live according to the Spirit.

Our body is the temple where our spirit dwells. 1 Corinthians 6:19 states, "Do you not know that your body is the temple of the Holy Spirit who is in you, whom you have from God?" Therefore we are to glorify God in our bodies and spirit. We should also maintain a balanced diet, exercise, and get the proper rest. This not only makes for a healthy body but a healthy soul.

Spiritual health, mental health, and physical health are essential for living a well-balanced life.

Affirmation: I am well-rounded. My mind and body are in perfect alignment. I live harmoniously.

Scripture References
Romans 8:1-11
Romans 12:1-2
1 Corinthians 6:19
Hebrews 5:14
1 Timothy 4:8
3 John 1:2

PEARL #78

Get Wisdom

The beginning of wisdom is this: Get wisdom.
Though it cost all you have, get understanding.
Proverbs 4:7 (NIV)

"Never mistake knowledge for wisdom. One helps you
make a living; the other helps you make a life."
Eleanor Roosevelt

Our social culture expresses the importance of a good education. But it is possible to be well educated and still lack common sense. Education gives us knowledge, but wisdom is a skill to apply knowledge. Wisdom coupled with application births understanding. It's one thing to be informed; it's quite another to be experienced.

The fear of the Lord is the beginning of wisdom. (Psalm 111:10) Wisdom is vital for everyday life. That's why Proverbs tells us, "Though it costs all you have, get understanding." (Proverbs 4:7 NIV) It may cost you time and money, but it is worth it. I wouldn't trade anything for the experience of life lessons. I don't believe you have to experience everything first-hand, but some things only come through experience. If we never had a problem, we would never know that God could solve them. It is through these times that we come to know God and know ourselves.

"If any of you lacks wisdom, let him ask of God, who gives to all liberally and without reproach, and it will be given to him." (James 1:5)

Affirmation: The more I live, the wiser I become. I am grateful each day for the experience.

Scripture References
Psalm 111:10
Proverbs 4:7
Proverbs 22:17
James 1:4-5

PEARL #79

Full Circle

That which has been is what will be,
that which is done is what will be done,
and there is nothing new under the sun.
Ecclesiastes 1:9

"The nature of God is a circle of which the center is
everywhere and the circumference is nowhere."
Empedocles, Greek Philosopher

Life consists of cycles. We are constantly evolving. Although there are many stages in the life cycle, they all come full circle. And so it is with all creation. The earth rotates around the sun. The ecosystem is naturally designed to evolve and start anew. Every twenty-four hours a new day starts. The numeric system goes to ten, then starts back at one. Even the products we purchase have a life cycle.

We were designed to progress. That's why it's so important to stay in alignment with God. When we are not aligned with our purpose, we get stuck in a cycle, and we find ourselves having to repeat it. God is never in a hurry when it comes to teaching us a lesson. We must learn the lesson so that we can move forward.

Other times something has come to an end in our lives, and God is preparing us for what's next. When something dies, it gives life to something new. Whatever the case may be, we need to evaluate why we are stuck. Is there a lesson you need to learn, or are you afraid to let go? Failure to move forward stunts your growth and compromises the life cycle. Be careful of stagnation. You were created to advance.

> *"The path isn't a straight line; it's a spiral.*
> *You continually come back to things you thought*
> *you understood and see deeper truths."*
> **Unknown**

Affirmation: I am aligning with God's purpose for my life. I am growing daily to become all He created me to be.

Scripture References
Job 26:10
Proverbs 8:27
Ecclesiastes 1:9
Isaiah 40:22

PEARL #80

A New Beginning

If anyone is in Christ, he is a new creation; old things have passed away; behold, all things have become new.
1 Corinthians 5:17

"Tomorrow is a new beginning. Embrace the light of a new day, for you have a fresh chance to begin again, to make a beautiful life."
Leon Brown

God loves us so much that even when we miss the mark, He stands ready to show us mercy and allow us a fresh start. When we come to Him with a sincere heart and confess our sins, He is faithful to forgive us of our sins and cleanse us from all unrighteousness. Not only does He forgive our sins, He remembers them no more. (Isaiah 43:25)

How refreshing it is to know that our Maker loves us so much that He paid the penalty for our sins before we knew we would commit them? This doesn't give us a free pass to sin, but it is comforting to know that He's not holding it against us if we make a mistake. "There is therefore now no condemnation to those who are in Christ Jesus, who do not walk according to the flesh, but according to the Spirit." (Romans 8:1)
New beginnings are not just for the young. As long as you have life, you have a fresh opportunity to begin again. You have another chance to carry out God's plan for your life.

He makes all things new. It's a new season. It's a new day.

Affirmation: I am thankful for a new beginning. I am ready for a fresh start.

Scripture References
Isaiah 43: 18-19
Isaiah 43:25
Romans 8:1
1 Corinthians 5:17

PEARL #81

Be Unstoppable

Do you not know that those who run in a race all run, but one receives the prize? Run in such a way that you may obtain it.
1 Corinthians 9:24

"She believed she could, so she did."
Unknown

"You can start late, look different, be uncertain, and still succeed." These are the words of Misty Copeland, a woman who made history in the world of ballet. Misty started studying ballet at the age of thirteen. That is considered late for this demanding form of dance. But she didn't let that stop her. She mastered the art of ballet and became the first Black woman to be the principal dancer for the American Ballet Theatre.

There is something about the way God made women. Women are brilliant, tenacious, and resilient. When we set our minds to do something, we are unstoppable. Women play to win.

This was such the case for a widow woman Jesus mentioned to His disciples. She went to an unjust judge seeking justice for herself from her adversary. The judge denied her for a while, but the woman was persistent. She refused to take no for an answer.

Though this judge did not fear God nor men, he eventually granted this widow's request so that her continual coming would not weary him. (Luke 18:1-5)

To be unstoppable is to know no limits. The only difference between winning and losing is to never quit. Giving up is not an option. You're not comparing yourself with others; you are blazing your own trail.

What seems to be in the way of you fulfilling your goal? Remember why you started and keep going.

Affirmation: I am determined. I am relentless. I am unstoppable.

Scripture References
1 Corinthians 9:24
Matthew 15:21-28
Luke 11:5-8
Luke 18:1-5

PEARL #82

Choose Contentment

I have learned in whatever state I am, to be content...
Philippians 4:11

"Be content with what you have; rejoice in the way things are. When you realize there is nothing lacking, the whole world belongs to you."
Lao Tzu

Contentment is like a lost art in the world today. We're addicted to achievement and having the latest new thing. We seldom take time to appreciate where we are by looking at what lies next. Greed and the need to have more are consuming our nation.

One way to surely lose contentment is to live from an outward view. If you solely depend on "the right" conditions or circumstances to make you happy, you will often be disappointed. Contentment is a choice. It is a state of being.

The secret to contentment can only be found in God. Godliness with contentment is great gain. (1 Timothy 6:6) We have to set our minds on things above. This involves spending time with God. The more time we spend with Him, the more we will discover the best things in life are priceless. In His presence, there is fullness of joy, and at His right hand are pleasures forevermore. (Psalm 16:11)

It's time to stop chasing things and start chasing God.

Affirmation: I am content in my heart. I am thankful for what I have and patient for what is to come.

Scripture References
Psalm 16:11
Proverbs 16:8
Philippians 4:11-12
2 Corinthians 2:15
1 Timothy 6:6-8
Hebrews 13:5

PEARL #83

Rejection or Direction?

*The stone which the builders rejected
has become the chief cornerstone.*
Matthew 21:42

*"If we live for people's acceptance,
we will die from their rejection."*
Lecrae

We often view rejection as a negative thing, but it could also be a blessing in disguise. There are many illustrations of rejection in the Bible. Take Joseph, for instance. Joseph was the youngest of twelve sons and was favored by his father, Jacob. As a result, his brothers despised him. They eventually sold him into slavery. But the Lord was with Joseph, and he became very successful. Joseph found favor in the house of his Egyptian master. His master went on to make him the overseer of his house and all that he had.

When a famine came upon the earth, Joseph was in a position to oversee the entire land of Egypt. People from near and far came to purchase food, including his brothers. Initially, he didn't reveal himself, but when he finally did, his brothers were afraid he would repay them for the evil they had done. But Joseph did not hold it against them. He told them, "God sent me before you to preserve a posterity for you in the earth, and to save your lives by a great deliverance. So now it was not you who sent me here, but God." (Genesis 45:7) Joseph now saw his brother's actions as direction, not rejection. He went on to say, "You meant evil against me; but God meant it for good, in order to bring it about as it is this day, to save many people alive." (Genesis 50:20)

Jesus was also rejected. "He came to His own, and His own did not receive Him." (John 1:11) He was despised and mistreated by earthly rulers, elders, and scribes. Yet, He remained humble and endured the cross. He was the stone, which the builders rejected, but He became the chief cornerstone. (Matthew 21:42)

Rejection is a natural part of life. But if we learn to view rejection as direction, we will see that God causes all things to work for our good. (Romans 8:28)

What may feel like rejection right now, may be God's direction. He holds our future and knows the path to get us there. (Job 23:10)

> *"You can't connect the dots looking forward; you can only connect them looking backward. So you have to trust that the dots will somehow connect in your future."*
> **Steve Jobs**

Affirmation: My steps are ordered by God. Rejection is course correction designed to direct me to my destiny.

Scripture References
Genesis 50:20
Job 23:10
Matthew 21:42
John 1:11
Romans 8:28

PEARL #84

Pruning Season

Every branch in Me that does not bear fruit He takes away...
John 15:2

"I will not violate God's standard for company."
Dr. Dharius Daniels

Have you ever let someone remain in your life who should have received their eviction notice a long time ago? We've all been there one time or another. Severing unhealthy ties is not an easy thing to do, but it is necessary. The worst is, the longer they stay, the harder it becomes to part ways.

In Luke 13, a man had a fig tree growing in his vineyard, but he did not find any figs when he went to look for fruit. He told the man tending his vineyard, "For three years now, I've been coming to look for fruit on this fig tree and haven't found any. Cut it down. Why should it use up soil?" The man replied, "leave it alone for one more year, I'll dig around it and fertilize it. If it does bear fruit next year, fine! If not, then cut it down."

I'm not sure what the man's reservation was for saving this tree, but you can tell he had become accustomed to it. It is so easy to keep holding on to something or someone way past its time. Instead of cutting the tree down as the owner suggested, he wasted time, energy, and resources trying to revive something that was never meant to be restored.

Take time to assess the relationships in your life. Are they bearing fruit, or are they just taking up space? Do they motivate you, or do they drain your energy? Be honest with yourself. Make up your mind to stop wasting time, energy, and resources on unfruitful relationships that no longer serve you.

> *There is a time for everything, and a season for every activity under the heavens... There's a time to plant and a time to uproot.*
> **Ecclesiastes 3:1-2 (NIV)**

Affirmation: Pruning is essential to my growth. It allows me to let go of anything that no longer serves me.

Scripture References
Psalm 1:3
Ecclesiastes 3:1-2
Luke 13:6-9
John 15:2

PEARL #85

The Master Vinedresser

I am the true vine, and My Father is the vinedresser...
and every branch that bears fruit He prunes,
that it may bear more fruit.
John 15:1-2

Cutting away branches that do not bear fruit sounds very logical. But in the pruning process, not only do the dead branches have to go, sometimes the vibrant ones must be cut back so more bountiful fruit can grow.

In a spiritual sense, our Heavenly Father deals with us in a similar way. He is the Master Vinedresser. He gently cuts away some things in our lives so that we can develop in one area or another. Many different circumstances may serve as His pruning knife. It could be a loss of interest in a particular person or thing, an irritation of some sort that continues to annoy you, or just an uneasy feeling on the inside that is telling you it is time to move on.

Allowing things to remain in our lives when they need to go can be detrimental to our growth. This was the case with Abram and his nephew, Lot. They both departed from Abram's father's house to a land that God was going to show Abram. During their journey, Abram and Lot's livestock grew to the point that the land could not sustain them, making it difficult to dwell together. This caused strife between Abram, Lot, and their herdsmen. As a result, a separation took place. Abram and Lot split ways, and Abram continued to prosper.

The Master Vinedresser knows what is best for us. We can trust His hands of precision as He cultivates us for His divine purpose.

Affirmation: My life is being shaped in the hands of the Master Vinedresser. I am being pruned to prosper.

Scripture References
Genesis 13:1-8
Psalm 1:3
Jeremiah 17:5-8
John 15:1-8

PEARL #86

The True Vine – Stay Connected

Abide in Me, and I in you. As the branch cannot bear fruit of itself, unless it abides in the vine, neither can you, unless you abide in Me.
John 15:4

As Jesus prepared for His earthly departure, He spent time with His disciples in an Upper Room. During that time, He revealed to them the secret to living the Christian life: "Abide in Me." He was letting them know that He is the source of life, and as long as they (the branches) stayed connected to The True Vine, they would experience a wellspring of life that produces fruit.

I love how God uses nature to illustrate how we are to conduct our lives. A vine is an essential point where nutrients flow. It serves as the lifeline to the branches. The nutrients freely flow from the vine to the branches allowing them to bear fruit.

"Abide" in Me is emphasized several times (See John 15:1-10). God knows our natural tendencies are prone to wander. It is so easy to revert to our natural abilities and intellect. But we should walk in a manner worthy of the Lord, fully pleasing Him: bearing fruit in every good work… (Colossians 1:10 ESV)

Be determined to abide in Christ. Stay connected to The Vine. He is the Source of life to all who abide in Him.

Affirmation: I am a fruitful branch connected to the Source that can never run dry. I will forever abide in Him.

Scripture References
Jeremiah 17:5-8
John 15:1-10
Psalm 1:3
Colossians 1:10
Hebrews 10:24-25

PEARL #87

Do the Work

Work out your own salvation…for it is God who works in you.
Philippians 2:12-13

Living a life in Christ is no small feat. Salvation is free, but if we desire to grow and mature in the faith, it will take some work on our part. God has a plan for our lives, but He will not force us to walk it out. We must be intentional in our pursuit of purpose. We have to work out what He put in us. (Philippians 2:12) This requires faith and discipline.

Faith and works go hand and hand. "For as the body without the spirit is dead, so faith without works is dead." (James 2:26) It is easy to have faith when things are working in our favor, but it is quite another to exercise faith when we can't see an end in sight. Things may start well, but as we continue, we may question, "Is this really what God wants me to do?"

This is where the struggle begins. We have to train our bodies to come into complete alignment with the perfect will of God. It takes time and discipline to strengthen our spiritual muscles. Developing godly habits will not happen overnight. There will be some fear, pain, and stretching. The work at times may seem mundane, but we have to work out our own salvation with fear and trembling without grumbling or complaining. (v. 12)

Do not lose heart. "Even though our outward man is perishing, yet the inward *man* is being renewed day by day." (2 Corinthians 4:16) And as we keep at it, we will learn to be led by His promptings. His will becomes our will. "For it is God who works in you both to will and to do for His good pleasure." (Philippians 2:13)

Affirmation: I am an outward expression of the inner work God is doing through me.

Scripture References
Philippians 2:12-13
2 Corinthians 4:16
Colossians 1:29
James 2:26

PEARL #88

Breakout!

See, I am doing a new thing!
Now it springs up; do you not perceive it?
Isaiah 43:19 (NIV)

"Your perspective will either be your prison or your passport."
Dr. Dale C. Bronner

It is a human tendency to focus more on our inadequacies than our potential. The sad thing is, some people stay there and pitch a tent. They began to think; maybe this is just my lot in life. They lose their zeal and their strength to fight.

The book of 2 Kings shares a story of four leprous men who lived as outcasts. They were sitting at the entrance of the gate of Samaria, which was their custom, but one day they had an epiphany. "They said to one another, 'Why are we sitting here until we die? If we say, 'We will enter the city,' the famine is in the city, and we shall die there. And if we sit here, we die also. Now, therefore, come, let us surrender to the army of the Syrians. If they keep us alive, we shall live; and if they kill us, we shall only die." (2 Kings 7:3-4) You have to read the rest of the story to get the outcome. I can tell you this... they were glad they went.

Do you feel stuck in a career, a relationship, or just in your own way? Life is full of stumbling blocks, pitfalls, and detours, but you cannot allow your current situation to keep you stuck! You must muster up the strength to keep going!

Self-doubt and fear come along with the territory. There will always be challenges and obstacles when you are pursuing purpose. But you cannot allow it to paralyze you. When life presents me with opposition, I focus on my "Why." My "Why" is the reason I do what I do. When your "Why" is big enough, it will cause you to push past whatever stands in your way.

God is doing a new thing, but it requires leaving your place of comfort to see it. Be resilient. Be relentless. Keep going! Breakout!

Affirmation: I see obstacles as opportunities to propel me forward.

Scripture References
Deuteronomy 1:19-21
2 Kings 7:3-4
Isaiah 43:19
2 Timothy 1:7

PEARL #89

Capacity

Jabez cried out to God, "Oh, that you would bless me and enlarge my territory!"...And God granted his request.
1 Chronicles 4:10

"Everything comes to us that belongs to us if we create the capacity to receive it."
R. Tagore

My father always had an aquarium for as long as I can remember. He started with guppies and goldfish and eventually purchased an Oscar. The person at the pet store told him that the Oscar could grow according to the size of the tank. My Dad had a 30-gallon tank, and we watched the Oscar grow tremendously.

Unfortunately, the larger he grew, the more he began to feel confined. He would bang his head against the top of the tank cover, trying to break free. There were a few occasions when he was successful. We would find Oscar lying on the floor, holding on to dear life. Each time this happened, we would place him back in the tank, placing a heavier object on top of the cover to prevent him from jumping out again. That worked for a while, but eventually, Oscar found a way to break out. Only this time, we were not home to save him.

Later, I discovered that determining fish growth by the size of their tank is a myth. Fish that don't grow to their fullest potential are either stunted or deformed. Research has found that many factors disrupt fish growth. But the primary cause is the pollution of water. When water does not properly flow and the proper filtration is not in place, it causes waste build-up. This build-up over time pollutes the water making the environment harmful, preventing fish from reaching their maximum capacity.

The right environment is also essential for our personal growth. Oswald Chambers states, "We must not measure our spiritual capacity by education or by intellect; our capacity in spiritual things is measured by the promises of God." God feeds us according to our capacity to receive. However, our sinful nature can interfere with us reaching our fullest potential. God desires to enlarge our territory, but He cannot do it if our hearts are polluted with sin. "Blessed are the pure in heart, for they shall see God." (Matthew 5:8)

Don't let the pollution of sin stunt your growth. Check your environment. Ask God to create in you a clean heart. (Psalm 51:10) When God knows you are ready, He will fill you to capacity.

***

Affirmation: I am in the right environment to grow and expand. I have the capacity to reach my fullest potential. God is enlarging my territory.

***

Scripture References
1 Chronicles 4:10
Psalm 16:6
Psalm 51:10
Matthew 5:6-8

PEARL #90

Poised & Positioned for Purpose

*Let us lay aside every weight, and the sin
which so easily ensnares us, and let us run with
endurance the race that is set before us…*
Hebrews 12:1

"The proof of desire is pursuit."
Mike Murdock

There is a certain position a runner takes when they are preparing for a physical race. To start, their attire is light, eliminating them of anything that would try to weigh them down. As they approach their places, they assume a low position. Their posture is in complete alignment. Their knees are parallel to the ground, their hands are precisely positioned, and their head is in the upright position. When the officials fire that gun, the runners dart off with force, with only one goal in mind—to cross the finish line.

The same applies to our spiritual lives. One must be poised and positioned to pursue purpose. Our attire is the garment of praise. Our position is the posture of prayer. Our eyes are set upward, and our hands, heart, and mind are open. Our goal is the prize of the high calling of God in Christ. (Philippians 3:14)

God is continually preparing us for the race that is set before us. If we desire to reach our fullest potential, we cannot be found getting ready; we must be poised and positioned–always in a state of readiness.

On your mark. Get set. Go!

Affirmation: I am poised and positioned to pursue my purpose.

Scripture References
1 Corinthians 9:24-25
Philippians 3:14
Hebrews 12:1
Revelation 19:7

APPENDIX A

Self-Discovery: Getting to Know You Exercise

*"Mastering others is strength.
Mastering yourself is true power."*
Lao Tzu

Life is full of teaching moments. God engineers situations in our lives in such a way that He reveals to us what we didn't know about ourselves.

When getting to know you, you discover things you like and things you don't like. You'll notice personal qualities you want to embrace and others that you may want to improve. You begin to identify your strengths and weaknesses. I call this the man in the mirror phase. This is the first step in getting to know you.

Remember, this is all about you right now. So take time to evaluate yourself. What do you like? Below are a few questions to get you started:

1. What is your favorite color?
2. What is your favorite season?
3. What is your favorite scent?
4. What kind of music do you like? Who's your favorite artist?
5. What is your favorite movie or TV show?
6. What is your favorite book? Who's your favorite author?
7. What type of activities do you like?
8. What do you enjoy doing so much, you lose track of time?
9. What is your favorite food(s)?

10. Are you an introvert or extrovert?
11. What are your strengths? What are your weaknesses?
12. What brings you joy?
13. What are your values?
14. What is your passion?
15. What are your triggers?
16. What makes you thrive?
17. What does your "ideal" self look like?
18. How do you reset, refresh and replenish?
19. What is one thing you want to accomplish before you retire?
20. List the people you admire and why you admire them.

Sometimes it's difficult to answer questions about ourselves because we place so much emphasis on pleasing others. By nature, women are able to adapt and modify our lives accordingly. Although this could be a good thing, we must make sure there is balance.

I encourage you to set up an appointment with yourself to complete this exercise. Learn to enjoy the company of one and get to know you.

Seek to be **YOU** even if that means being misunderstood.

APPENDIX - B

The Power of Affirmations

An affirmation is simply a statement declaring what you believe to be true. God used His words to speak the world into existence. In one declaration, life was formed. And since we are made in His image and likeness, He has given us the authority to do the same.

The book of Proverbs teaches us that death and life are in the power of the tongue. When you release words into the atmosphere, they begin to take shape. Your words are either working for you or against you. Words matter, so choose them wisely.

Below are 31 affirmations for your use. Select a few that you would like to apply in your life. Feel free to tailor them to your liking. Read your affirmations aloud each morning and rehearse them throughout your day. As you dedicate time to this practice, you will develop a habit, which will become a lifestyle.

1. I commit my works unto the Lord, and my thoughts are established.
2. I awake each morning with great expectations. The possibilities are endless.
3. I am rooted in God's word. Wherever I am planted, I will flourish because I was made to prosper.
4. I have an inner peace that cannot be disturbed.
5. I am wise and make good decisions.
6. I am grateful. I learn to see the good in everything.
7. I am unstoppable. The only limits that exist are the ones I set.
8. I am determined. I accomplish anything I set my mind to do.
9. I am magnetic. Positive energy flows through me. I attract what I truly want.

10. I am spirit-filled and spirit-led. I live to pursue God's purpose.
11. I am pliable. I am teachable. I am growing. I am learning. I am a work in progress.
12. I am bold and courageous. I take risks. I either win or learn.
13. I am resilient. I see obstacles as opportunities.
14. I make time for self-care to refresh and replenish my soul.
15. I embrace change and welcome new ideas that help me to evolve.
16. I am creative. God wired me with ingenuity.
17. I am qualified and equipped for my God-given assignment.
18. I am being renewed and transformed daily into the image of Christ.
19. I am in a constant state of overflow. Rivers of living water flow through me.
20. I am living my best life. I am taking in the goodness of every given moment.
21. I am becoming. I embrace who I am as I evolve into the best image of me.
22. I am mindful of my mental, physical and emotional well-being. I engage in activities that keep me healthy.
23. I am a woman of influence. I walk with dignity, grace, and self-respect.
24. I am rare and authentic. I live my life unapologetically.
25. I am a trailblazer. I set trends and show people what's possible.
26. I am becoming better acquainted with myself and learning to do what's best for me.
27. I am learning and developing at my own pace. I march to the rhythm of God's drum.
28. I am the exception to the rule. I am called to raise a standard.
29. I am an ordinary woman called to do extraordinary things.
30. I am governed by faith, not feelings.
31. I am blessed with family and friends. My network is my net worth.

Resources

Below are a few books and websites that have helped feed my faith and inspired me to live each day fulfilling my purpose.

Understanding the Purpose and Power of Woman – Dr. Myles Munroe
Repositioning Yourself – T.D. Jakes
The Path Made Clear – Oprah Winfrey
The Purpose Driven Life – Rick Warren
My Utmost for His Highest – Oswald Chambers – www.utmost.org
Our Daily Bread Devotion – www.odb.org
BibleGateway – www.biblegateway.com
Abide Meditation – www.abide.co

About The Author

Doreen Ellis is a Lifestyle Writer who inspires readers to live life on purpose. Her new project, *Pearls to Purpose: A 90-Day Women's Guide to Self-Discovery* is filled with life lessons on living a life of freedom and fulfillment. She believes we all were created for a purpose, but it starts with knowing who you are and being comfortable in your own skin.

Doreen was always different from her peers. God set her apart at a very young age. She tried her hardest to fit in, but she always stood out. It took some time for her to come to that realization. However, once she did, her purpose shone through and she began teaching others how to embrace their uniqueness and live an authentic life unapologetically.

Doreen has a Bachelor's Degree in Marketing from Kean University. She is a wife, mother, coach, and mentor, who enjoys writing, taking nature walks, traveling, and spending quality time with her family.

She is also the Founder and CEO of Pursue Purpose, LLC and Casting Pearls, Inc., a non-profit organization designed to educate and empower women socially, spiritually, physically, and financially. Her mission is to develop well-rounded women who know who they are so they can pursue their purpose. For more information visit www.DoreenEllis.net.

Linkedin: https://www.linkedin.com/in/doreen-ellis/
Facebook: https://www.facebook.com/doreen.wellsellis
Instagram: https://www.instagram.com/iamdoreenellis/

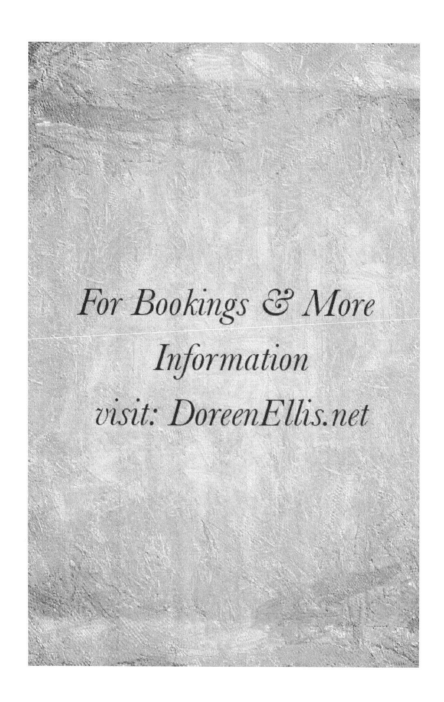

For Bookings & More Information visit: DoreenEllis.net

Made in the USA
Middletown, DE
14 May 2022

65633003R00115